About boomerangs
America's Silent Sport

by Kelly Boyer Sagert

Here is the first definitive work on this quietly
olympian sport and its poetic, almost spiritual,
attraction to throwers around the world.

PLANT*Speak Publications

About **boomerangs,**

America's Silent Sport

© Copyright 1996 by Kelly Boyer Sagert

Cover Design by Don Sagert of A Write Impression
All photographs by Leonard J. Burns,
unless otherwise credited.

Format and Printing by Elyria Graphics, Elyria, Ohio

ISBN 0-9646803-3-5
First Edition, First Printing

A PLANT*Speak Publication
All Rights Reserved
34100 Center Ridge Road
North Ridgeville, Ohio 44039
216-327-5059

Dedication:
To Don, Ryan and Adam, my wonderful family,
and to Lynn, a wonderful friend.

Acknowledgements

Many thanks to every boomerang enthusiast who helped me, because without that generosity, this book wouldn't exist. And, a special thank you to six boomerangers, who went far above and beyond the call of duty.

First, to Gary Broadbent, a true friend and inspiration. His enthusiastic and energetic style of throwing introduced me to this sport.

Next, to Chet and Gregg Snouffer, who have shared endless amounts of information over the past couple years, spending hours on the phone and at the computer for me. To Michael Girvin and John Flynn, who trusted me with their truly precious boomerang collections.

And, to Ted Bailey. His engineering knowledge and dedication to precision gave me the confidence to write this book. His generosity is truly overwhelming.

And, of course, many thanks to my husband, Don, and my sons, Ryan and Adam, for their patience, and for their willingness to eat plenty of fast food. Thanks to Len Burns, the ever ready photographer, and to my family members and in-laws who baby-sat for me and encouraged me.

To my sister, Tracy, who listened to endless revisions and crazy ideas while I wrote this book. To my friends at the America On Line Writers Club and to my friends in every day life.

While my name appears on this cover, it seems a little unfair, because this book is truly a group effort.

iv

Contents

An Opening Dialogue vi

History - from the Flying Stick to the Boomerang 1

Profiles: Pioneers, USA and World Champions
    Chet Snouffer 9
    Ted Bailey 15
    Gary Broadbent 19
    Eric Darnell 24
    Mike Dickson 27
    Doug DuFresne 29
    John Flynn 32
    Michael Girvin 35
    John Gorski 39
    Steve Kavanaugh 41
    Bob Leifeld 43
    Moleman 45
    Barnaby Ruhe 48
    Adam Ruhf 51
    Gregg Snouffer 54
    Mark Weary 57

Profile of a Typical Rang-er 60

Weapon: Fact or Fiction? 63

How To Toss Like a Pro 64

Tournament Events 72

Talk the Talk - Boom Glossary 76

Records: World and American 78

Making Your Own Boomerang 79

The Physics of Boomerangs 80

The Art of the Boomerang 86

Women in Boomeranging 99
    Betsylew Miale-Gix

Booming Around the World 107

A Note on Virginia Beach, 1996 111

Boomeranging Resources 112

A Closing Dialogue 120

Publishers' Comment 121

About the Author vii

An Opening Dialogue

"Hey, did you check out Air Gorski's floater yesterday?" the man called out to the woman. "He's really shredding lately."

The woman cupped her ear to hear the man over the wind. She remembered him from the practice field yesterday, and he looked like a really dedicated boom competitor.

He had to be talking to her, because they were the only two people practicing in this crazy weather. It was hard to hear what he said, but he was probably asking her for some throwing advice. "Looks like your rang just blew by," she shouted back. "Keep it vertical, by the way — and use your Tri-fly®!"

The man couldn't believe it. Was this woman actually trying to tell him how to throw? Him? He'd competed in boom tournaments all across the country, without any of her help, thank you very much. "Everybody's a critic," he grumbled, picking up his swiss cheese Omega instead.

"Watch this, then," he said to the woman, as he moved a little closer to her, picking a point just slightly higher than the horizon. "I guarantee you'll see a real rippa!"

The woman yawned. Geez, not another one of those kind of guys. He acted like Babe Ruth pointing his bat towards the stands. "You think you're such a boom stud," she said. "It'll just be another blow-by."

By now, the man was irritated with this woman. She sure didn't need to have such an attitude, not when he was only making conversation. "What makes you such a boom babe?" he asked, his hands on his hips.

"This," she said, whizzing a fast catch boom out twenty meters in the opposite direction of the man, then snagging a one handed catch. "About three or four seconds, wouldn't you say?"

The man was impressed. "Wow! That was incredible," he said. "Maybe you should be giving me some tips."

"You're as good as I am," she said, walking towards him. "That was an awesome dingle arm throw you made out there, by the way. I'm just nervous about tomorrow, competing against Gel, Chet the Jet, Broadboom, the Moleman and Chi Bob. This is my first national."

The man laughed, and he nodded his head in agreement. "I know what you mean. I'm afraid I'll toss some grounders tomorrow, while they make the raddest catches ever. I'm not even sure I want to try the Aussie Round or the MTA."

"Yeah, we'd better work together, instead of arguing," she agreed, figuring this guy wasn't so bad, after all. "What about adding a little flapage to the boom? Have you tried a humpback throw?"

History -
from the Flying Stick to the Boomerang

To unravel the twisting, turning history that spun itself through the previous conversation, you'd have to travel back in time. You'd slip back into an age before there were airplanes, before there were cars, before the signing of the Declaration of Independence.

You'd travel to a place where America wasn't yet known, to a time long before William the Conqueror subdued England in 1066. You wouldn't even recognize the world you'd enter, the primitive, murky horizons of ancient man. You'd keep whirling until you time travelled back about 20,300 years, spiralling down into a cave in the Oblazowa Rock of Southern Poland.

While crouched down in that shadowy cave, you'd watch a man losing his precious stick, one that he had stone fluted from a tusk captured in the great mammoth hunt. His throwing stick would huddle in that cave for century upon century, dirt and rocks gently layering themselves on top of his once prized possession, burying it over the ages.

The stick would rest there, until archaeologists unearthed the shattered artifact, revealing their priceless find in 1987. Carefully piecing it together into a gently curving shape, scientists believe that the many scratches on the ivory were etched during the life-time of the mammoth itself. The stick was found beside an ancient thumb bone, the oldest human remain found in Poland, possibly the thumb bone of that ancient warrior, he of the great mammoth hunt.

Now, as you leave that fascinating cave, ease back into your imaginary time machine, and continue your journey through time and place. Spinning closer to home, move forward in time by about 10,300 years. There, you'd see an oak stick, carved about 10,000 years ago, only recently uncovered in Florida.

If you glided forward in time by about another 4,700 years, maybe you could solve a puzzle, one recently uncovered by archaeology student Thomas Stehrenberger. While digging around Lake Konstanz in Switzerland in 1996, he discovered a similar type of stick, one that appears to have been thrown away before it was finished, while still in the midst of fabrication. How did that stick get broken, precisely at that point, somewhere around 3300 BC?

Whirling forward by about another 1,300 years, you would witness the creation of golden-capped, carved ivory sticks, and dark,

Oldest known throwing stick, 20,300 years - Poland

1

gilt-tipped ebony sticks, handcrafted in Egypt around 2000 B.C. Those sticks dazzled the scientists and explorers who discovered them in 1922 in the now famous Egyptian tomb of King Tut.

During your amazing time travels, you'd also peek at a small cashew wood stick left in an ancient Indian cave in Brazil, surrounded by ceramic scraps and broken bones, only recently uncovered. Brazilian Indians incrusted alligator, piranha or jaguar teeth into their sticks, for increased power; so, during your travels back in time, you might see them insert those teeth before covering their sticks with a protective layer of the milky fluid of the rubber tree.

During your lightning fast scan of the globe, you'd find these sticks used in India, Africa, the Netherlands and Europe, as well. The Hopi Indians of North America called theirs "rabbit sticks," the skill for creating them passed on by their ancestors, the Anasazi Indians.

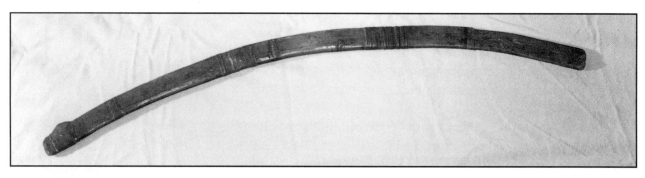

800-year old "Rabbit Stick" S. W. Native American

4-Blade Chinese Top Cross Stick design (Modern version)

A four bladed Chinese top cross stick existed before 1300 AD, more than 700 years ago. No one knows how many more of these sticks remain hidden, or in what country they will surface next.

Now, it's important to reserve time to land on a secluded continent, that of Australia. At this time, you'll need to spin your time machine into reverse, once again spiralling back into time.

Aborigines whittled throwing sticks in Australia as long as 10 to 20 thousand years ago. And, while you're gliding down in long ago Australia, it would be a good time to figure out what all these sticks were used for, and to speculate on why they appeared all over the globe.

All peoples around the earth, throughout time, obviously have needed to eat. As hunters and gatherers, they also needed to find an efficient way to hunt. One of the earliest meat gathering methods was the throwing of sticks and stones, and this style of hunting probably developed independently throughout the world.

And, since you're visiting ancient Australia, take a moment and watch these hunting masters at work. Observe those long ago aborigines, and the skills needed to throw their slightly curved, almost banana shaped sticks, now known as kylies.

During your trip through time, consider yourself lucky if you get to watch an expert aborigine bringing down an animal with his powerful, three-foot sidearm killing swath. His stick was heavy, probably thrown at about 60 mph, and it may have had a nasty hook on one end.

After completing the job, however, the hunter had to run to retrieve his precious stick. While his stick could fly, it could not return to the thrower. It was not a boomerang.

Amazing stories have centered around these powerful sticks. One aboriginal legend claimed that the wife of one of those warriors was kidnapped from a rival tribesman during a terrible storm. The warrior huddled by his fire, cold and hungry and angry about his missing wife. By the third day, he was so furious that he grabbed the stick he used to build his fire, and he threw it as hard as he could. Not only did that frighten away the storm, the stick brought back the warrior's wife. She returned, with a big fat turtle for dinner. He never forgot what his suddenly magical stick did for him, and so he held on to it forever.

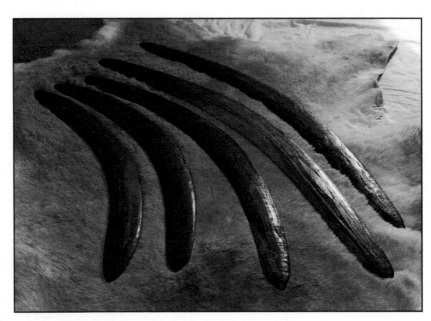

Now, while the rest of the world changed their style of weaponry over the centuries, turning to spears and bows and arrows, men on the isolated land of Australia kept making better and better sticks. The thick forests of Europe demanded a more efficient hunting weapon, while in the more open plains of Australia, the kylie worked just fine.

Early Throwing Sticks. Note curved construction, minimal angles

Also, many two legged animals are native to Australia; so, a throwing stick that damages one of two legs brings down the animal for the hunter. For those countries with plenty of four legged animals, one hurt leg is not enough for a hunter to bag his prey, another reason weapons needed to advance.

But here is where more exact science leaves us, and educated speculation steps in. As wanderers, the Australian aborigines travelled with their worldly possessions heavy on their backs. Not wanting to carry any more weight than absolutely necessary, they carried few tools except for the versatile kylie. Kylies were used to dig roots, to search for water, to sharpen tools and to scrape smoking ashes off of roasted game.

The aborigines also used the kylie to create a musical sound. They twirled them, thumped them and tapped them to make music, using them in ritual ceremonies.

Over time, the stick probably smoothed down to a trailing edge, creating a stick with one flat side and one curved side. The primitive people probably delighted in the slight lift and turn in flight that their sticks now achieved.

Pulling up the misty curtain of time, it's easy to imagine a man carving a smaller stick out of a lighter wood for his young son, instead of using the heavy, dense black wattle wood that he reserved for himself. The son may not have understood the importance of a sidearm throw, which cut a wide swath, and therefore was more likely to bring down a fleeing target. So, the young man may have even thrown his stick vertically.

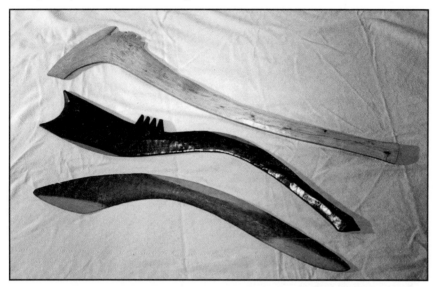

Early weapons, not boomerangs

Again, what a marvelous extra lift in flight his stick had! Although those long ago people didn't realize it, by making a smaller boomerang, their stick had a much more efficient flight lift to it.

Those sticks may have had natural curved elbows in them, similar to those found in tree limbs. When a young man killed his first kangaroo with a smaller but stronger stick, he probably carefully rubbed the kangaroo jaw along his stick. By doing so, he believed the powerful kangaroo spirit was imparted into his weapon. The tough teeth and bone of the animal grooved the stick, causing a strange stability to enter the throwing stick.

These sticks began to hover in a circular path. It was probably not long after the discovery of this unusual trait that the aborigines put the sticks to more efficient use. They took advantage of the magically circular spin of certain throw sticks. Tossing them over bodies of water thick with bird life, they noticed how the birds huddled under the whirling object, an object that now miraculously returned to the thrower. These returning sticks, perhaps the first real boomerangs, imitated a predatory bird in the sky, so the lake fowl gathered protectively together under the stick, an easy catch for a hunter with a net.

So, the returning boomerang was born. Whether it first happened in Australia is still a point of controversy, the answer obscured in the haze of time. While Australia is traditionally known as the birthplace of the returning boomerang, some modern day researchers are finding contradictory evidence.

Jacques Thomas studied replicas of the Egyptian sticks found in King Tut's tomb, for example, and he was impressed with the returning abilities of some of them. He wrote a fascinating book on his findings, called **The Boomerangs of a Pharaoh**.

Thomas has a technical background, serving as a military pilot in the French Air Force. (He also enjoys the excitement of boomerangs, starting a French boomerang club. He is working on re-opening a boomerang museum, and he once threw a boomerang across the international date line in a Supersonic Jet.) Thomas isn't the only modern day boomerang investigator, however.

M. Ingen Housz made a replica of an ancient Dutch throwing stick that was created around 300 BC, and discovered in 1962. Housz has experimented with the replica of the oak stick, finding it to have excellent aerodynamic abilities.

But, since so few well-preserved ancient sticks have been discovered, it is difficult to identify with certainty where the first returning boomerangs were created. While the oldest true, returning boomerangs created in Australia are thousands and thousands of years old, the sticks may have been better preserved in the climate of that continent. Australians may also have simply continued to use the soaring sticks long after others had discarded them. In any event, we have to thank those long ago aborigines for preserving and safeguarding this magic for modern men and women. And so, unless you'd like to share new information you've gathered during your time travels, the question of where the first boomerang was created is still debatable.

One thing is certain. Confusion spread when the great sea-faring explorer Captain Cook arrived in Botany Bay, Australia in 1770. He saw the natives wielding carved sticks, some of which had the remarkable ability to return when thrown. When the explorers first spotted those marvelous sticks, Cook and his crew must have been amazed. Ignorant of the aborigine language, Cook asked the Australian natives what their curved sticks were called. It was a tough question, because the aborigines filled their language with lyrical terms for each type of stick they used. Colorful examples include "nanjal, baranganj, kali, wilgi, barngeet, and tootgundy." So, when the aborigines answered Captain Cook with the word sounding like "bou-ma-rang," he assumed that all thrown sticks were called boomerangs.

Perhaps more harmful than misinterpreting the name of the mysterious returning stick, however, is that Captain Cook had unwittingly lumped together the kylie and the boomerang. Kylie sticks were dangerous weapons. Boomerangs, on the other hand, were used as decoys, as entertainment, and as a part of ancient ceremonies. Thus, the terrible myth of boomerangs as weapons began.

Myth-clothed as it was, after Captain Cook's discovery, the boomerang certainly had arrived in civilization. As the Dublin University Magazine pointed out in February, 1838:

> "Of all the advantages we have derived from our Australian settlements, none seems to have given more universal satisfaction than the introduction of some crooked pieces of wood shaped like the crescent moon, and called boomerang or kilee. Ever since their structure has

been fully understood, carpenters appear to have ceased from all other work: the windows of toy shops exhibit little else; walking sticks and umbrellas have gone out of fashion; and even in this rainy season, no man carries anything but a boomerang; nor does this species of madness appear to be abating."

And, as Mark Twain observed in 1897:

"Either someone with a boomerang arrived in Australia in the days of antiquity, or the Australian aborigines re-invented it. It will take some time to find out which of these two propositions is the fact. But there is no hurry."

During the first two hundred years since Captain Cook broke the news about boomerangs, the bent stick has had its moment of glory. The first American boomerang factory opened in 1904 in Topeka, Kansas, according to the Topeka Capital Journal. The time was ripe for a flying toy. Americans were fascinated with the efforts of the flying machine recently invented by the Wright brothers. The boomerang factory employed between 30 and 35 people, and they claimed to have had over one million dollars worth of business in 11 years, selling 25 and 50 cent boomerangs. The factory operated until 1924.

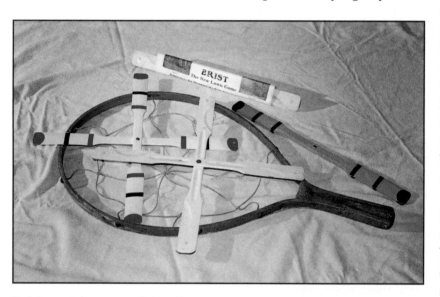

Brist game (rare complete set)

During that time, boomerang inventor Sam Brist demonstrated his boomerangs. In a booklet published in 1903, he claimed that if you would have shown your friends your throwing skills a century earlier, "you would have been tried and convicted of witchcraft." Then, when his game of Brist was announced, the company claimed that the game "will go down in history as the most wonderful novel invention of the age."

In Brist, each player was given three boomerangs and one Brist Rakah, a small circular net used to catch each boomerang upon its return. The players stood in a bullseye type design, earning points if they caught the boomerangs in their Rakahs, in the correct area of the bulleye.

While the game was considered more popular than croquet for a short number of years, the game eventually died out, and boomerang throwing was almost extinguished in America.

Then, in 1968, Felix Hess, a physics student from the University of Groningen in the Netherlands started to throw and calculate the flight patterns of a boomerang. Using lighted boomerangs, he took night time pictures tracing the action of flying boomerangs. He eventually earned his Ph.D in 1973 after publishing a weighty thesis called *"Boomerangs: Aerodynamics and Motion."* Travelling to Washington DC in 1969, Hess threw a boomerang that circled the Washington monument, and soon after, the sport of American boomerang throwing was born.

Benjamin Ruhe, a man who had lived in Australia during part of his two year "vagabond walkabout" years earlier, started a boomerang toss at the Smithsonian Institute in 1969. About 600 people signed up in the first 48 hours, according to Ruhe's nephew and throwing-mate Barnaby Ruhe. Ben Ruhe went on to sponsor 13 annual boomerang tossing tournaments, making American competitive boomerang throwing more widely known.

Over the years, Ben Ruhe greatly promoted the fun and enjoyment of boomerang tossing. He preferred casual competition, as his adopted rule from the *Mudgeeraba Creek Emu Riding and Boomerang Throwing Association* shows:

> *"Decisions of the judges will be final unless shouted down by a really overwhelming majority of the crowd present. Abusive and obscene language may not be used by contestants when addressing members of the judging panel, or conversely, by members of the judging panel when addressing contestants, unless struck by a boomerang."*

Then, in 1981, an American team coached by Ben Ruhe was bold enough and talented enough to challenge the Australians to a contest. Travelling down to Australia, the upstart Americans swept all three matches, sparking a friendly competition that has evolved into the multinational competitions of today.

Always searching to improve, to innovate and to compete, almost two extraordinary decades have passed since that first two-country match. While the Americans lost a rematch with Australia in 1984, they have been undefeated in all international team competitions from 1985 until a second place finish behind Germany in 1996.

American ingenuity and skill have acted as catalysts to make these world competitions a stage for innovations of design and technique, and for truly spectacular championship competitions. The list of participating countries is growing, with the following countries sending teams to New Zealand in 1996 for the international, Olympic-like competition: America, Germany, France, Switzerland, New Zealand, Australia, Italy, Canada and Japan. While American dominance in the sport was challenged in New Zealand by the French and German teams, the American champions you'll meet in the following pages plan to continue to use their talent, energy and skill to hold on to their competitive edge.

Time Line

30,000 BC	18,000 BC	8,000 BC	3,000 BC	2,000 BC	300 BC	2,000
THEN <───> NOW						
1	2 3		4	5	6	7 8 9

1 - 20,300 years ago - the year when the oldest throwing stick was discovered in Southern Poland.

2 - 15,000 years ago - the age of the Australian Cave Paintings, showing boomerangs.

3 - 10,000 years ago - the year when a throw stick uncovered in Florida was estimated to have been crafted. It also is the time of the oldest returning and non-returning boomerangs found in the Wyrie Swamp peat bog in Australia. Those boomerangs ranged in age between 7,900 and 10,200 years old. Australian Geographic, in 1988, stated that the stick was probably in Australia 40 to 50 thousand years ago, although none of these have ever been found.

4 - 5,300 years ago - the year when a Swiss throwing stick was probably broken during fabrication.

5 - 4,000 years ago - the year when exquisite throwing sticks were created for King Tut, some found to be excellent returning boomerangs.

6 - 2,300 years ago - the time when a Dutch boomerang, found to have excellent returning abilities, was created. It was also about the time when Anasazi Indians carved non-returning rabbit sticks for hunting in the desert area where Arizona, Colorado, Utah and New Mexico meet. About 1,000 years later, their descendants, the Hopi Indians, continued the craft in northeastern Arizona.

7 - 700 years ago - the time when a four-bladed Chinese top cross stick was created.

8 - 226 years ago - the year 1770, when Captain Cook traveled to Australia, learned of boomerangs and kylies, confused the two, then brought the mixed-up information back to England.

9 - **Now**, the most exciting time to ever, ever throw a boomerang!

✦ *Chet Snouffer*

Delaware, Ohio

AKA "The Michael Jordan of the Boomerang World"
AKA "Chet the Jet"

Boomerang throwers all across the country - - no make that the world — whisper the name Chet Snouffer in awe. No wonder. Chet snags boomerangs in the midst of powerful backflips, he juggles 502 boomerangs in a row in just forty five minutes, and even more importantly. . . He is the highest ranked thrower in American boomerang competition history, wearing the world championship crown a record three times. He earned that honor in Paris in 1985, in Washington DC in 1989 and in Hiratsuka, Japan in 1994.

His USA records may never be broken. Chet has been the national champion ten times, again the most times in American history. Chet has led the United States International teams to victory a record seven times, participating in the historic 1981 victory over Australia.

While Australia snatched victory from the United States in the rematch of 1984, the American team has been unbeaten in international competition from their victory in 1985 until their second place finish behind the German Young Guns in New Zealand in 1996.

In 1995, when Chet earned the world championship title, he had already won the US Open, as well, making him both national and international champ at the age of 38. In 1994, Chet's name was added to the Who's Who in the Midwest, and by 1996, he graced the Who's Who in the World. Featured on PM Magazine, ESPNs Amazing Games, CBS Nightly News, Australia's "Who" Magazine, MTV Sports and Sports Illustrated, he is modest about his accomplishments.

"Sometimes when I'm throwing, I'll be transported back in time, like it was the first time I'd ever thrown a boomerang, and I'm absolutely amazed at the flight of it," he said. "I'll have a weird moment of disbelief too, when I watch a lefty throw, and I'm fascinated by the opposite flight of the boomerang."

Chet Snouffer
10-time
USA National Champion

"Boomerangs are a passport to the world."

9

Chet's fascination with the enchanting returning stick actually started when he was ten. After reading a Reader's Digest article about boomerangs, he and his grandfather made a successful boomerang from a piece of leftover panelling in his parents' basement. Later, during his years at Wheaton College, he became known as the boomerang man, and by 1979, his life of boomerang competitions had begun.

In 1981, at age 25, Chet was the youngest member of the upstart American team, that group of people who flew to Australia to challenge the best throwers in that country to a competition:

"It was a dream come true for me," Chet recalls, "throwing in the motherland of the boomerang, and hanging with the all-time greats. These were all the guys I'd only read about in books, and now I was throwing booms with them in the first international comp ever. Wow! Incredible."

And, how did Chet survive his trial by fire? By scoring more points than anyone on either team, that's how. "That really boosted my confidence," he said, "and I began to believe that I, too, could become one of the greats if I applied myself."

Chet almost didn't fly to Australia in 1981, however, hurting his arm a week before the plane left. Practicing for the tournament on an unusually warm Ohio day in November, he separated his right shoulder diving for a catch. "I felt that with one week to go, I wasn't going to able to throw," he recalled.

Calling one of his coaches, Ali Fujino, he said, "I hurt my arm, I can't go."

Ali replied, "Get on that plane."

Chet headed to the doctor, who prescribed medicine and a week's rest. "So, arm in sling and taking horse pills, I went. We no sooner landed, jet lagged out of our minds, than the Australians whisked us off to a local school for a demo."

Okay, first throw in a week. How did it feel? "Perfect," he said. "No pain."

Such are the circumstances of great historical moments. Chet was part of the pioneering team, that unassuming group of throwers who thought they were just good enough to challenge the Aussies. And he tossed a 40 out of 50 in the final Aussie Round event, to put them over the top for the USA's first international victory.

What could possibly be next for this rising boom star? In 1982, Chet was one of a small number of people gathered under a tree on the polo field at the Mall in Washington DC. Under that tree, this select group created the United States Boomerang Association, electing Carl Naylor the first president.

The organization still exists, with Chet the 1996 president of the USBA. A father of two young children, Chet is also a gymnast, a gymnastics coach and a gym club owner. He travels extensively, performing for youth, encouraging a drug-free lifestyle.

And, he still makes many of his own boomerangs. " I firmly believe each thrower should build his own boomerangs," Chet said, "because therein lies the magic. Your boomerangs and your throwing style merge and become one over time."

"I love boomerangs because they're unique, they don't make noise and they don't pollute," he added. "You don't have to build stadiums or destroy natural beauty to play. With boomerang throwing, there are no court fees. Instead, you can go to an open space, and entertain yourself for hours. That's the satisfaction and the beauty of the boomerang."

The uniqueness of the sport is also what originally attracted Chet. "By doing this, I set myself apart, and that was an instant attraction to me when I started out." "You know," he continued, "I can pull over in a park anywhere, pull out some booms and instantly meet people. I couldn't do that with a football or a basketball." He adds, "It's a passport to the world, an instant conversation piece, an ice breaker, and a chance to give something away and get someone else excited. "

While Chet amazes people everywhere he throws, his throwing style has also earned the respect of other boom tossers throughout the country, including Mike Dickson who explains the boom phenomenon known as the "Chet winds." Apparently, even on a windy day, the strong breezes die down when the master thrower Chet Snouffer steps into the throwers' circle. "Chet can read the wind, and he sees 'windows of opportunity'," Mike said. "He has necessary mental toughness and the confidence, as well."

"Chet is an incredibly gifted, excellent athlete," said another fellow thrower, Steve Kavanaugh. "He is absolutely the most consistent, best thrower in the United States."

"Having Chet Snouffer on your team improves the team one hundred percent," said 16 year-old thrower Adam Ruhf. "He's a great captain, always practicing hard and staying focused. He's truly the best ever, like Michael Jordan when he's in the zone."

Chet Snouffer gets good height on this difficult trick catch.

"You just don't see Chet make mistakes," Adam added. "He's also like a great baseball pitcher who knows he needs one more strike in the ninth. Chet just won't bomb out."

And, like a successful baseball pitcher, Chet adjusts his throwing to the situation. "I credit my ability to adjust and finesse throw in a variety of conditions with part of the success I've had," Chet said. "When a baseball pitcher only has one or two pitches, he's easy to hit. Throwers who have just one style of throw are going to encounter winds and situations to which they have difficulty adjusting."

He believes another key to successful throwing is the ability to move quickly. "That suits my style," he added. "I end up working a lot less because when I get going, I'm not just moving around, I'm focused. That way, you stay fresher physically and mentally."

Chet considers why so many Americans do so well in boomerang competitions. "We have access to great materials, including good woods and plastics," he said. "Besides that, we are gregarious self-promoters, with at least a dozen of us with the entrepreneurial spirit to make our living off of boomerangs."

"Americans, too, are very competitive and pragmatic," he added. "We want to win, we want to be more effective. We don't stay contented with what we have or know, but instead we're constantly improving our equipment, our technology and ourselves. We'll do what we have to, in order to pull out a win."

Chet sums up his own winning attitude this way. "I go into every tournament believing I can win. I've been in enough situations to realize that I can do what it takes, regardless of the score at the moment or the caliber of the competition."

Comparing early competitions to more recent ones, he comments, "In the early years, I felt like I was competitive because I trained harder and threw more than anyone else. As time went by and guys were training harder, I felt like it was my experience that gave me an edge, but the important thing is that I learned and believed that if I worked hard enough and made the right choices, I could win."

Chet's brother, Gregg, points out that Chet never allows his successes go to his head, however. "Even though for six years, Chet won every domestic tournament in which he competed, he can recount each national title, and the situation that allowed him to pull it off, paying respect to the throwers who have made it difficult for him over the years."

Chet retired temporarily in 1994, although he couldn't stay on the sidelines for long. "Maybe I just needed a break, some time to let somebody else be on top," Chet said. "You know, I wouldn't make a good boomerang champion if, at some point, I didn't try to make a comeback."

He competed in the US Open in 1995, winning the tournament. The US Nationals follow the next day; three times in the past, Chet had won the two tournaments back to back. "I wanted to honor what I said in 1994, though, that I wouldn't do this again," he said. "It was no fun, winning the biggest tourney of all and then having to go out there the next day to prove it again."

Chet said that by *not* throwing in the 1995 Nationals, it paved the way for his future throwing. "I had finally come to the realization that I didn't have to prove it again," he said. "That was a big turning point for me, a huge personal growth, because prior to that, I had felt I had to keep winning titles. Every title, to affirm my place in the history of the sport."

"To actually sit out and not even attempt to defend the title was the turning point that allowed me to "unretire" and feel the fun of throwing again," he added. "Now, I'm excited about throwing and I want to make the 1998 team that regains the world title!"

So, what does this champion thrower think about the second place finish to Germany in New Zealand? "You always learn more when you lose, and we lost to a great team," he said. "The main lesson I learned is that you can't win all the time, but it's better to be there playing than not."

Chet placed sixth in the individual world championships in New Zealand, in a close competition. "I knew that if I didn't compete, there would definitely be a new world champion," he said. "By going and participating, maybe you win and maybe you don't, but your only shot to win is to play."

He always throws to the best of his ability. "If you win, you realize it was good enough compared to the others, but you always have to wonder whether they did their best or maybe they made mistakes. As the defending champion, when you lose, you're always assessing whether the others have passed you by or whether you're still in the game and simply got beat that day."

Chet shares one last story, one that he calls a "cool lesson you get when you least expect it."

While throwing at a demo with his six year old son, Cody, and fellow thrower Gary Broadbent, Chet threw his custom made *Herb Smith* weighted hook boom. "On the return, it swooped over the fence behind me, and disappeared with a distant 'metal on rock' thud out of sight behind some trees," he said. He thought local residents were kidding when they said there was a 200-foot cliff behind the fence, but no, they weren't kidding.

After 20 minutes of hacking away at briars and thistles, and scrambling along the base and face of the rock wall, Chet came to a realization. "Without Divine intervention, I was never going to find this rang." This was no ordinary boomerang, either. The one of a kind design was created for Chet for the 1989 World Championships, where Chet snagged the world title in Washington DC. The creator of the boom had since died, making the boomerang all the more precious.

"Praying for guidance to find the rang, I pondered what lesson I might possibly be supposed to learn from this," he said. "Here I

Chet adds this about the 1996 German win. "It will make international competition more exciting, encouraging everyone in the sport."

13

was, helping my buddy Gary, and I lose a priceless stick!" Climbing up the difficult rock, Chet saw his son, Cody. "He was sitting in the middle of the field, waiting for his Dad, while Gary was merrily selling every boom in his bag to the crowd."

"Just one look at Cody, and I realized - - this boomerang isn't nearly as important as that little guy out there," he said. "While I might stay down here all night looking, maybe the lesson I'm to learn is to let it go, to put people first over the object. Sounds simple, but when you're as crazed about boomerangs as Gary and I are, you realize this is going to be an incredibly painful lesson when ol' Chet leaves the rang behind."

"Like lightning, I realized Gary needed to hear this as much as I did," he added. "I decided then and there to walk away, to tell Gary that people are more important, that we were leaving the boomerang."

Then, wham!

There was the boomerang, lying at his feet. "I had stood there pondering for five minutes, but I never saw it until I let it go," he recalled. "Goosebumps ran over me, and I grabbed the rang, hiding it in my shirt."

He shared with Gary the lesson he had learned. "He looked dazed and confused, trying to grasp the idea that I was leaving that boom behind," Chet said. "Then, I whipped out the rang, and told him it was there all along, but I couldn't see it until I was ready to walk away."

"Some say finding the boomerang was coincidence," Chet added. "Those who know better, however, smile and understand."

✦ Ted Bailey

Ann Arbor, Michigan

One of this engineer's many contributions to the boomerang world is his definition of the boomerang, his phrasing now officially accepted around the world:

Boomerang: *Number of arms is unrestricted. To be a boomerang, a stick must tend to return as a result of gyroscopic precession caused by asymmetric lift. The lift is created as a result of a throw that gives the object rotation and linear motion. An object that is thrown from the hand, unaided by any mechanical means, with a combination of both translation and rotation about its center of mass so that gyroscopic precession (caused by differential lift over the airfoil surfaces relative to its angular orientation) and aerodynamic lift combine to produce a flight path that returns the boomerang to the thrower or within a reasonable distance from the thrower.*

Ted Bailey with his revolutionary-design MTA.

Wow. While previous definitions of the boomerang tended to focus on the appearance of the flying stick, Ted took a different approach to the question, and instead he revealed how the magic of boomerangs worked.

His idea was first accepted by the United States throwers, and then an engineer, Dennis Maxwell from Australia, with tiny modifications, put his seal of approval on Ted's definition. The rest of the world quickly agreed after that.

Ted is the unofficial historian of the boomerang world. I've interviewed dozens of people for this book, and countless numbers of times I've asked a question and gotten this response. "Hmm. . .I don't know the answer to that, but I know someone who would. His name is Ted Bailey, let me get you his phone number. . ."

I posted e-mail messages throughout the Internet, and got this reply. "Hey, you've just got to talk to Ted Bailey, okay? Here's his e-mail address. . ." I checked out the boomerang newsletters, and what name did I see over and over again on the bylines of intriguing articles? That of Ted Bailey.

So guess what I did? I talked to Ted Bailey. My husband Don, and Len, the book's photographer, made a weekend long journey to Ted Bailey's house, starting their own personal obsession with the flying stick.

Len's response to the visit explains Ted's wealth of knowledge far better than I could. "Kelly," he said, "there's enough stuff here for a thousand page book. No, make it more than that."

A week later, I accompanied my husband and Len to Ted's house, for even more boom photos, folklore and info. Nothing was ordinary at Ted's house. Each boomerang had an incredible legend behind it, and when we left, we were shaking our heads at Ted's encyclopedic knowledge, his absolute genius. Ted's mother had gifted him with his first boomerang when he was nine. Tossing it around, it didn't work well at all. While walking to school one day, he threw his ineffective boomerang, smashing a nearby window. After being chased for more than a mile by an angry, obscenity filled man, Ted gave up boomerangs for many, many years.

While in college, lefty Ted started fooling around with a cheap plastic boomerang, another one that didn't return. Discovering that the boomerang wouldn't return in the hands of a left-hander, Ted built a wooden mirror image copy of the boom, and his boomerang flew and returned.

Throughout the 1970s, Ted knew of no other throwers, so he tinkered with his boomerangs with little assistance. When finally he discovered the enormous amount of information on aerodynamics available in NASA technical reports, however, Ted's creative, innovative mind took over, and the rest is history.

Competing from 1982 until 1989, Ted won several tournaments in 1985; in fact, if he didn't win an event, he placed in the top ten in almost every event he entered throughout his competition years. "I frequently took first place in specific events because of technologies that I created," Ted said. "I was the first person to ever do Super Catch and the first to throw and catch an MTA that was documented with a flight over one minute, and then I caught the first one that flew over two minutes, as well."

Hmm. . . MTA.

Ted's name is almost synonymous with MTA technology, MTA being the competition level sport where a boomerang must stay in the air for as long as possible. A special, hockey stick shaped boomerang is tossed for this event. More details of the event, formally known as Maximum Time Aloft, will show up in later in this book, but here is how Ted radically improved the technology of the boomerang used in MTA.

Ted found a reference to an MTA-type boomerang being patented as early as 1895. It wasn't until the late 1970s, however, when an actual event called *Duration* focused on keeping a boomerang in the air for an extended period of time.

By 1980, Ben Ruhe's Boomerang Newsletter mentioned the Maximum Time Aloft event, with Barnaby Ruhe spinning a flight of 20.24 seconds. Meanwhile, European Wilhelm Bretfeld was experimenting with large boom models that flew for more than thirty seconds.

While Bretfeld greatly improved the MTA technology, Ted started scaling down the boomerangs. After he had successfully created a smaller version of the Bretfeld boomerang, Ted was sailing his improved MTA for more than a minute.

"I was responsible for the miniaturization craze in the early 1980s, by making tiny, wind resistent boomerangs that were not only functional, but advantageous to use in competition," he said. "As a result, most boomerangs today are much smaller than they were fifteen years ago."

Ted used his knowledge of the smaller, more effective boomerangs, and integrated that with the then-current MTA technology. "I integrated the smaller size with a new shape, and I invented the twist and bend tuning that everyone uses today," he said. "Before my MTAs, most MTAs were flat and large with lead weights and undercutting. I put an end to all of that."

The event has since been broken down into two categories, MTA and MTA 100. With the regular MTA, the time counts whether or not the boomerang returns to within 100 meters of the original throwing spot. With MTA 100, the rang must be caught within that range to count. While the unlimited MTA is drifting away in favor of the MTA 100, Ted hopes there is room for both events in today's boomerang world.

Okay, now let's back up a little. Ted was seriously involved with MTA technology, but he was also the first to do Super Catch? What is Super Catch?

Consider it the boomerang thrower's trial by fire. First, the thrower tosses an MTA boom in the air. Then, the thrower must toss out and catch a boomerang, known as a "fast catch" boomerang, five times in succession with each of the five throws going out at least twenty meters. All this before the MTA spirals down. All this, plus the thrower must catch the descending MTA, or the whole event is kaput.

Ted points out that the thrower must toss the fast catch rangs from the same spot as where the MTA was launched. "This makes the event even more difficult," he said, "because you need to run the distance the wind blows the MTA, in order to catch it."

But difficult? Hah! Ted laughs in the face of difficult. He was told repeatedly that the feat could not be accomplished. On August 29, 1986, during a term as USBA President, Ted decided to attempt the Super Catch in calm weather conditions. He tried three times; on his fourth attempt, as darkness threatened to fall, Ted caught five fast catch throws in just 26 seconds, leaving about six seconds to catch his MTA.

"I was elated," Ted said, in a 1986 interview. "I knew I could do it. It was just a matter of trying again and again."

He created two techniques that allowed him to be the first to achieve Super Catch status. First, after throwing the MTA, he paused for a couple of seconds, to prepare himself for a different throwing style. Second, another person watched the MTA in flight, so Ted would know where to run for his catch.

Three days after his first success, Ted completed three Super Catches. "Given the right conditions and two perfect rangs," Ted said, "Super Catch is almost easy."

Ted's importance to the boomerang world goes far beyond his impressive throwing and technological skills, however. Other more recent contributions have included several years of editing **Many Happy Returns**, the official United States Boomerang Association newsletter, along with creating and editing *Boomerang News* and the *Boomerang Journal*. "I also supply boomerang databases and other computer shareware," Ted said.

He was featured in a book, called **NASA: Spinoff 1992**, in the section titled Technology Twice Used, Spinoffs in Consumer/Home/Recreation. In it, they said, "Boom designer and thrower Ted E. Bailey pioneered the use of NASA aerodynamics technology in boomerang shaping and he became one of the sport's leading innovators."

After that book appeared, Ted demonstrated a one minute plus MTA flight for CNN, and the segment aired around the world. Ted received letters about it from as far away as New Guinea.

He is one of the few people in the world who can give an exact technical explanation of why a poorly performing boomerang isn't working, and an exact solution on how to correct it. For that reason, along with many others, Ted was recently elected as chairman of the newly formed **World Boomerang Association**. "The goal," Ted explained, "is to make this a real, viable organization within one or two years."

Dr. Fredric Malmberg, a well known creator of artistic boomerangs said he respects Ted's scientific and competition contributions. "I'm glad you've talked with Ted," he told me. "He is one of the real pillars in this group, and he's a great guy, too."

And, thank you, Dr. Malmberg, for reminding me of Ted's other sterling qualities. While Ted is boom history, while Ted is boom technology, he also appreciates the sheer beauty of the boomerang. His private collection includes antique boomerangs and kylies, along with beautifully crafted inlaid wooden boomerangs from around the world.

If there is a well known boomerang designer, craftsperson or artist, Ted has one or more of those boomerangs. If there is a new boom crafter who shows promise, Ted has one of the newbie's earliest attempts. If there is an important historical twist in the boomerang world, Ted has solid, physical evidence of it in his collection. The bottom line here? If you need to know, just ask Ted.

✦ Gary Broadbent
Canton, Ohio

AKA Broadboom
AKA The Doublemeister

"Boomerangs are the most ferocious, bodacious, vivacious, gregarious, low to the ground, hard to bring down, bobbin' and weavin', shakin' and bakin', stoppin' on the dime and leavin' nine cents behind, number one, second to none sport in the world."

BOOM STEPPIN'
(A Poetic Tribute from Bud Pell)

I STEPPED ON GARY'S
FAST CATCH BOOM.
NOW I GIVE HIM
LOTS OF ROOM.

*Gary Broadbent,
Entrepreneur Rang-er*

Gary does nothing, absolutely nothing, part way. Life, according to Gary, is to be lived to the utmost fullest, and Gary himself often seems larger than life. While many boomerang throwers have one or two or ten or twenty boomerangs, Gary has over 10,000, ranging from antique throwing sticks to unusual, colorful boomerangs of his own design. He proudly wears a t-shirt reading, *"He who dies with the most boomerangs wins. . and I'm winning, I'm winning!"*

While he creates cartoon-like boomerangs for his collection, he also owns an astounding number of antique kylie sticks and boomerangs, each with their own unique tale.

Spotting an especially shiny kylie, Gary held it up, saying that natives treated their wood with the oil of a guana lizard, a protectant that could last for hundreds of years. Picking up a swan necked kylie, with a sharp triangular peak on one end, Gary held it up to his face. "Picture an aboriginal woman, skirted with emu feathers," he said. "She'd hold this up to her face, like a beak, and the inquisitive emu birds would circle around her. Then, pop! She'd get dinner."

Then, he clacked together lighter sticks, making ceremonial

music. He displayed another stick, with the original red ochre paint still on. He described an intriguing "message stick," where someone carved out animals and footprints, possibly directions to a long ago hunting ground.

While in New Zealand, Gary heard about throwing sticks that were used as "passports" from one tribe to another. If you didn't have the proper stick, and you were in another tribe's territory, you could be in serious trouble, according to Gary. So, they traded their sticks, allowing one another safe passage into each other's territory.

Gary then spun around an intriguing solid piece of wood, called a bull roarer, an oval shaped piece of wood, with two pointed ends, on a rope. The bull roarer made an eerie, whistling sound. "Picture how far in the distance you could hear this in the days when there were no television sets, no radios and no car horns," Gary said. "It could have been used as a signal, or part of a ceremony."

Even boomerangs and kylies originally made for commercial purposes have a place in Gary's extensive collection. He showed us two sticks featuring carved emus. Made in the early 20th century by aborigines, they were often sold to soldiers. "Even though they were made so the aborigines could make money, they're now an important part of the history," Gary said.

Holding up a decorated, squiggly shaped boomerang made by Australian boomerang legends Les and Arthur Janetzki, he explains why this boomerang was nicknamed Skippy. Apparently, there used to be an Australian television show about Skippy the Bush Kangaroo. Gary describes it as an Australian Lassie type of program. In one episode, Skippy gets bitten by a snake, which inspired the Janetzki brothers to create the Skippy boomerang in a snake shape. The boomerang is far more beautiful, however, than its quirky origins might suggest.

Gary recently purchased electrical equipment, planning to create boomerangs that light up like stars in the night sky. And now, I've probably touched on a thousandth of his collection. Maybe. Or maybe not quite.

While most US competitors took three team shirts to New Zealand, Gary took eighteen. He also handed out 130 t-shirts there, the shirts proclaiming that you need to *do what you love, love what you do, and the world will come back to you, like a boomerang.*

The German team told Gary that when boom fans die and go to heaven, they'll end up at Broadbent Boom Boot Camp. Another person referred to the Broadbent Institute of Booms. "I'm so obsessed with boomerangs," Gary said, "that I'm continually conscious of the wind, even when I'm not throwing, even when there are no visible signs of the wind."

Even more incredible, however, is this: Prior to his New Zealand trip, Gary headed to Australia, where he taught a group of aboriginal elders how to throw boomerangs. "I thought I'd died and gone to heaven," he said. Gary and Australian champ Bruce Carter

One of Bud Pell's poems seems particularly appropriate for Gary:

"NO MORE COUNTING"

AS BOOMERANGS GO,
I CERTAINLY HAVE MANY
AND FEEL SORRY FOR THOSE
WHO DO NOT HAVE ANY.
I REMEMBER THE TIME
WHEN I HAD ONLY ONE.
NOW, IT SEEMS LIKE
I HAVE MORE THAN A TON.
NO MORE DO I COUNT
EACH ONE EVERY DAY,
I JUST USE A SCALE
TO SEE WHAT THEY WEIGH.

headed out to visit an aboriginal culture center in Melbourne. While there, they met three men who were descendants of the aborigines who tossed long ago rangs.

"While these men had seen boomerangs thrown years ago, they didn't really know much about them," Gary said. "I took them out onto a field, and pulled out my bag of competition boomerangs. They were a little suspicious of those that weren't the traditional two bladed shape, so I demonstrated those."

"I thanked them for their culture," he added, "telling them that I believe their ancestors created the most amazing invention of anything throughout primitive times."

While there is certainly much to envy about the experiences Gary has had, life hasn't always been easy for him. He became a single father of his five small children after his divorce, with three of his children in diapers, two of his children ill with cystic fibrosis and his twins under one year old. He was a salesman for Campbell's Soup Company, selling to about 40 different stores on the east side of Cleveland. While the job was lucrative, he had little time to spend with his children.

Broadbent with his signature "Colossal Boom"

Not one to sit around and complain about life, a real lemons to lemonade kind of guy, Gary took a leave of absence. Then, he boldly went one step further.

"My parents couldn't believe it when I said I was quitting my job to stay home with the kids, and to work with boomerangs," Gary said. "They said 'it's just what we need in our family — *a boomerang thrower!*' " Gary set up a booth at a craft show, stood up on a chair and started tossing his small boomerangs around his booth. Soon, the awestruck crowd was ten deep, and Broadbent Boomerangs was officially on its way.

After his boomerang business took off, his family has been supportive, and Gary now makes, sells and throws boomerangs full time. Married to Vera, their children now number six, and the number is growing. (Number seven arrived in September, 1996.)

A self-admitted obsessive-compulsive boomeranger, the love of the sport almost literally spills out of Gary. "Boomerangs are coming back," he says. "Live to boom, and boom to live!"

Time flies for Gary while he throws. "When you toss with Gary," thrower Mike Dickson said, "forget real world time. Now you're on Gary time."

Vera explains it this way. "As long as you remember that a "Gary five minutes" equals a half an hour for anyone else, you should be okay."

While Gary absorbs all he can from life, he also gives back everything he can, generous with his time, knowledge and skill. "Truly, any boomerang enthusiast is welcome at my house, to make and throw boomerangs," Gary said. "You know that." I certainly can testify that I've felt welcome any time I've visited his house. When I first starting writing for the *Lorain Morning Journal*, in 1993, the editors asked me to come up with a feature idea, a profile of someone intriguing living in Lorain County.

I panicked. I had volunteered to play kickball with the church Bible school that night, leaving me little time to come up with a feature story idea. Then, between innings, (or whatever you call those things in kickball) my minister's wife suggested that I call Gary Broadbent, saying he was known throughout the boomerang world. Her son and an exchange student from another country had recently spent a day at Gary's house, making and throwing boomerangs, and they had come away highly enthusiastic.

I now admit to feeling a little nervous as we drove to Gary's house for the newspaper interview. This man had set world records, and he was going to talk to me? From the moment I walked through his front door, however, I felt like we were old friends, that I'd been there a hundred times before. So, yes, I know he means it when he volunteers to help any boom enthusiast who needs a jump start in the sport.

Gary shares his boom skills in schools throughout the state of Ohio and beyond. Tossing a kylie stick the entire length of a football field, he makes a goal. Then he throws a wildly painted boomerang, then another, his famous "Colossal Boom" measuring four feet from tip to tip. Whizzing a boomerang at the speed of 100 mph, he also catches boomerangs behind his back, with his feet and in rapid succession. He intrigues youth with his amazing boomerang feats, dazzles them with his enthusiasm and charisma and wows them with his zest for life. "Wouldn't you love to just throw boomerangs in a park all day for a living?" he asks. "Isn't this great?" By this time, the students are all but up on their feet. "Yes! Boomerang throwing for a living! Yes!"

"Do you know how I'm able to do all that?" he then asks them. " I went to school, stayed in school and I earned a degree in physics. With that knowledge, I was able to create boomerangs." He offers a powerful stay in school message. " If you stay in school, you'll be able to do work that you really love," he says. "If you do work that you love, you'll never really work again. If you do work that you love, you'll be controlling life, instead of life controlling you."

Gary has set many national records, along with four world

records, and he competed in the world boomerang tournament on the international team in Japan in 1994. Attaching sparklers to boomerangs, he performed a dazzling light display in the darkened stadium there, his boomerang performance art captured by CNN cameras. He also competed as a member of Team 1 in the 1996 World Tournament in New Zealand.

He finds boomerang throwing the ideal sport. "With boomerangs, you're both the quarterback and the receiver," he said. "It's a great sport to play with friends, or something you can do by yourself. Each boomerang has its own personality, just like people do."

He also emphasizes the athleticism needed to rise to the top. "People often say boomerang throwing is the lazy person's sport, since the boom comes right back to you."

Wrong.

While a baseball pitcher throws perhaps 75 to 100 pitches in an hour, according to Gary, a boomeranger throws that many times in 5 minutes during the endurance event. After they throw, they often run to catch the boom, having to stop on the dime to make a spectacular catch. "You need endurance, stamina and speed to throw boomerangs," he said.

Gary, along with other top American throwers are continually striving to improve their boom skills, their daring style often in contrast to more conservative throwing displayed outside the country. "Our team saying is *you don't fantasize, you mantisize*," he said. "The praying mantis is our team mascot, because they're always very hungry, trying to catch anything and everything. They're extremely fast and always up to a challenge."

He points out the wide variety of boomerang appeal. "It's a science, a craft, a hobby, a sport, a competition and an art. I'm happy, prosperous and successful, loving what I'm doing. Life is good."

✦ Eric Darnell

Vermont

"When you throw a boomerang, you're throwing into the unknown. You're throwing into a wind you haven't felt yet, your boomerang feeling the gust before you do. It's like waltzing with a 'rang, a dance where the wind is your silent, or not so silent partner. While other throwers consider the wind their nemesis, I think of it as a sometimes hard to communicate with kind of friend."

It finally happened. The American Team took second place in the international competition in New Zealand, in 1996, after twelve years of international domination of the sport. The German Young Guns rose to the top. And what did that powerful German team do when they won? Rub it in the faces of the Americans? Laugh about it behind their backs?

Eric Darnell,
Inventor of the Tri-fly®

No. Instead, they asked Eric Darnell, an American thrower of long standing to officially consider himself an honorary member of their team. "They said that without my boomerang technology, they couldn't have won," Eric said. "They'd studied my equipment since 1989." This was the second major compliment paid to Eric by that team. In 1995, the German throwers flew Eric over to their country, to honor him for creating the best boomerang ever made.

So, what is this magical piece of technology that has impressed top throwers around the world? Eric Darnell created the Tri-fly®. Darnell's revolutionary boomerang smashed any notion that a good boomerang needed to be two bladed in order to really fly. Darnell's boom has three wings.

Eric's boomerangs have been used to set over twenty-five American and world throwing records, including the current national and world fast catch records. Few throwers anywhere in the world have dedicated so many years to the perfection of the boomerang. This dedication with flight started when he was a toddler, after he started flying in airplanes with his father when he was just three years old. As soon as he was able, he began trying to create his own flying objects, making gliders out of balsa wood.

" I got discouraged, though, because after all that work, the glider often flew away after one flight, never to be seen again," he said. "Then, I saw a boomerang in an encyclopedia, and I loved the idea of wings that returned."

"My dad bought me a clunky boomerang that was just ridiculous," he added. "I knew that I could make a better one myself." It took Eric a year to create one that flew to his satisfaction. Then, in the early 1970s, Eric read an article in the Wall Street Journal about Benjamin Ruhe and his boomerang workshops, and the boomerang tournaments held at the Smithsonian. After writing to Ruhe, Eric received plenty of archival information on boomerangs. He also received an invitation to Washington D.C., and Eric participated in and easily won several events during the next Smithsonian boomerang tournament.

After these victories, he began experimenting with the various shapes of boomerangs, hollowing out the underside, adding bulbous tips on the end, adding holes to the wings, and painting them in easily spotted neon colors. "If you can hear a boomerang whizzing closer, but you can't see it, you can feel pretty queasy," Eric said. "I was the first person to make the boomerangs that you could easily see in the air, in the snow, in tall grass and in the trees."

The holes in the Tri-fly® greatly increased the boomerang's ability to return in low wind conditions. The holes did not, however, decrease the boomerang's flight-quality on windy days. Then, Eric made the first indoor boomerangs. He used foam, and then he made the first out of plastic. Pause here. The importance of a plastic boomerang is far greater than it first seems. Plastic boomerangs are adjustable.

"You can adjust a plastic boomerang before each flight, tuning them to adjust their rates of hover and range," Eric said. "They can be used for both left and right handed throwers, too." Not everyone immediately accepted the idea of plastic boomerangs, but Eric was used to defending his rangs. "When I first started competing in tournaments, I wasn't even allowed to take my boomerangs on airplanes, because they thought of them as weapons."

He had one close call when travelling to compete in Switzerland. "They made me put my boomerangs in the holding compartment, and then they lost them," he said. "Four days later, they showed up, just in time for me to compete, and to take second place in the tournament."

Boom technology remains Eric's main preoccupation, however. "I've competed only grudgingly," he said, "although I've managed to set two world records, and I've participated on all the American international teams except for the 1994 trip to Japan." He added, "I was in Japan in spirit, though, and of course, my boomerangs were there."

Eric was the Captain of the *Masters Team* in New Zealand in 1996, a team comprised of the pioneers of modern boomeranging. "The ideal international situation will be when we have at least four teams that could win, all the way until the end," he said. "We need a more level playing field." Darnell notes, "Americans have the advantage of knowing how to play as a team." He acknowledges, "It's important to continue supporting your teammates, for example, even after you may have destroyed your own personal round in an event."

Darnell believes that the German Young Guns pulled out their win in 1996 because of their improved team play. "They practiced together, as a team, for a month before the tournament," he said. "We need more teams doing that, so there is excitement over who will win a tournament, right up until the very last day."

He enjoys coaching youth, and he participates in throwing workshops. One boy in particular sticks out in his mind. The boy had faltered during the first two events, but Eric saw something more in him. "I went over to him, and told him I thought he could be one of the ten quickest in the fast catch event," he said. "The boy was intimidated, but I took him through, step by step. It was great watching him go towards success."

Eric defines success as feeling a sense of accomplishment. "The boomerang is absolutely still magical for me," he said. "You throw an object as hard as possible, away from yourself, and it comes back." "Of course," he continued, "the real magic always happens when no one else is watching," he added, tongue in cheek. "I always say everything is possible — in practice."

Eric has appeared on Discovery channel, as they followed him to Australia, filming him during the 1988 International Competition. He has designed the helmet lacrosse players wear, an equestrian saddle, soccer equipment, martial arts protective equipment and a wood burning stove that is marketed throughout Europe.

He created an ambidextrous boom, and he can throw two boomerangs at once, holding one in each hand, tossing them across his body, his arms forming an "x" shape at the release of the rangs. "After forty years, my heart still speeds up when I watch a boomerang in the air," he said. "It's still exciting, and I still can't fully describe the beauty of one in flight."

"You don't have to be crazy to throw boomerangs," he added, "but it helps."

✦ Mike Dickson

Canton, Ohio

AKA The man with the injury that was felt around the world.

"I thrive on the competition and getting together with compadres to throw, but there still is nothing like the relaxation of what I call 'field meditation' -just me and some time to throw and to think, to think about each rang, each throw, each new rang just made; figuring out old ones, getting into a groove, just throwing myself into a zone."

"What happened to Mike? Have you heard?"
"No, what kind of injury do you think it was? I just wish I knew."

That's just a sample of the conversation that flew around the Internet and over telephone wires after a message got back to the United States that Mike Dickson of US Team 1 was injured in the world tournament. "I pulled a hamstring, and I could only run at about 50 percent capacity," Mike told me after he returned to the United States. "While that was disappointing, New Zealand was still an amazing experience. Throwing boomerangs together is an international bond that cuts across nationalities."

While he has always been an athlete, attending college on a tennis scholarship, Mike didn't start competing in the boomerang world until 1990, at the age of 36. "Part of the challenge of boomerangs is adapting new technology to your throwing style," he said. "Whether you make or buy competition booms, you still need to flap, tune, weight and adjust the boom to your throwing style; that is, the particular angle and speed of release, to make the boomerang your own, and to make it work for you."

Mike Dickson
USA Trick Catch Record Holder

"Boomerangs are like snowflakes, " Mike says, "with no two, not even of the same model, being exactly alike. You need to search for the boomerang that will jive with your throwing style. Competitive throwers have a kit bag with a boomerang for every range, every speed and every event."

Mike competed in three tournaments in 1990, and he has been ranked in the top ten list of American throwers in every year since 1992. And, he's only getting better; in 1995, he was just one half of one point away from a fourth place finish. In 1995, he also tied the world trick catch record, snagging 31 unusual catches in a row. "l was also ready to create new history in 1996," he said.

He even enjoys practicing his sport. "Like any creative endeavor, each session is a learning experience," he said. "Each time, you learn more about the boomerang, and it is a growing, creative experience."

"Looking from the inside out, I can't understand why everyone isn't fascinated with the boomerang," he added. "Throwing and catching a boomerang is intrinsically satisfying, a simple act that just feels good." He ponders the paradox of boomerang throwers; while a friendly, outgoing, let's-get-together-from-all-over-the-planet kind of group, they are still highly self-sufficient and individualistic people.

"At one tournament, Chet Snouffer looked around and noticed we were each eating our lunches alone," Mike said. "While we are all compadres, we are also our own people." The very nature of the sport encourages that trait, according to Mike. "Boomerangs pit you against nature," he said, "and it's up to you how well you do. You can really blaze your own trail."

He wonders about the future of this grass roots sport. "I always kid around that our children will be negotiating their boomerang contracts, while we did all this for free," he said, with a laugh, "but I also say -who needs money when you've got boomerangs?"

Mike hopes that more people start participating in tournaments, preferring to attract more active participants to the sport instead of worrying about the small number of spectators. "This sport is not going to go away," he said, inviting others to join in. "Now is the time to take an interest in it, to be one of the real pioneers of boomerangs."

✦ Doug DuFresne

Portland, Oregon

AKA The man who threw lighted boomerangs at night, and ended up having the police called in to investigate a UFO sighting.

"With boomerangs, opponents are also your friends, sharing their ideas with you on how to throw and how to make a better boomerang."

Doug DuFresne dislikes rules, but he dislikes someone having an unfair advantage or disadvantage even more. "If a boomerang competition isn't fair," he said, "If the results aren't fair, then it isn't fun." Doug has spent almost twenty years throwing boomerangs, including participating in the 1981 tournament in Australia. From the beginning, he has enjoyed the friendly competition of the sport.

"I credit Dennis Maxwell, a member of the 1981 Australian team, for creating the friendly, upbeat tone of international boomerang competitions — and others," Doug said. "As emcee during the first contest in Melbourne, he cheered and congratulated members of both teams with genuine enthusiasm for their achievements. Because of that, the sport has evolved into a sport where friends compete — not against each other so much, but against natural and personal limits, and against the wind."

*Doug DuFresne
Member of USA 1981 Australian
Challenge Team*

And, he also credits the 1981 Australian team. "Although their national pride was at stake, and although they were serious about the competition, they greeted us at the airport and treated us like royalty." The 1981 meet had three "tests," or matches. "About two thirds of the way through the first test, coach Ben Ruhe called a meeting, and told us that it was possible for us to win! It was amazing the effect that had on us," Doug said. "We thoroughly expected to be taught a lesson in boomerang throwing by the Australians. We were shocked to find that we could compete at their level and actually win!"

Although the Americans won all three matches, they ran into one - no make that two - little problems, both of whom will live on in boomerang folklore forever: Between the three main matches, the American team tossed against local throwers, beating them as well. While in Albury, however, they were greeted by two brothers, Les and Arthur Janetzki each about 5 foot, 3 inches tall. Amazingly, they were both around the age of 80. Even more astounding than that, they competed on the only local Australian team to beat the powerhouse Americans!

The Janetzki brothers had earlier tastes of fame, while headlining as vaudeville performers in Australia and New Zealand in the 1920s. Along with brother Harold, they created a xylophone and soft-shoe dancing routine, and they were the specialty act that accompanied an early movie titled *"For the Term of His Natural Life."*

The advent of talking movies convinced the Janetzkis to switch to the grocery business. They weren't involved in boomerang throwing until their retirement. After spotting a combination butcher and boomerang shop in Albury while in their sixties, however, they became intrigued.

After teaching themselves how to throw the rangs, they began making high quality boomerangs from the plywood from which shipping cartons were made. Les glued two 1/8 inch thick pieces of plywood together to make 1/4 inch, 6 ply plywood. Then, he cut the blanks out and shaped them with files. Arthur finished them with about 40 layers of shellac, decorating them with gorgeous aboriginal-style designs.

Les, at the age of 84, snagged an individual championship in Accuracy at the Barooga-Albury Open, beating out four members of Australia's National team. Arthur, only 81 at the time, took second place in Aussie Round, often called the most difficult competition event. Their trademark used to be clicking their heels after they left the field. While Les died in 1987 at the age of 86, Arthur only recently died in 1995 at the age of 91.

"Les and Arthur seemed surprised that we had all heard of them," Doug said. "They lived with their sister, Ruby. The three Janetzkis were extraordinarily pleasant, polite and accommodating towards us — and towards each other."

"One image that remains in my mind is of 6 foot, 7 inch tall Al Gerhards with Arthur and Les on either side of him. These were three boomerangers of similar stature in the boomerang world, and with similar dispositions, but of significantly different physical stature."

"I thought it interesting," Doug added, "that the Janetzkis had no power tools. Their workshop was simple, and impeccably clean. Meeting them was an awe inspiring experience."

Since that time, Doug has participated in most international competitions, tossing on the USA Masters team in New Zealand. Meanwhile, his wife Diane has contributed an enormous amount to the sport, as well. "In 1985, Diane attended the nationals in

California, and within an hour, she jumped up and volunteered to help out. The throwers really appreciated it, and now she has been a judge or head judge at most of the international meets," he said. "The team cups have been dictating all our vacations since 1988."

He compares the tournaments. "During early tournaments, we didn't even know what events would be contested before the tournament started, and the rules might change in the middle," he said. "Our desire is to have interesting, fast-moving tournaments that are fair, and that use the same events and rules. This allows us to compare throwers for national standings and team selection."

Doug works full-time on his boomerang passion, creating and selling 'Outback Boomerangs.' "Diane tests the novice ones for me, since she isn't a serious thrower," he said. "She'd taught school in Australia for three years, yet she'd never seen a boomerang thrown until she met me at a boomerang contest in Portland."

"Boomeranging is great because age and gender don't matter, " he said. "There are no significant limits on boomerang design. You're free to experiment, try new shapes, materials and technologies, and to make boomerangs that suit your personal throwing style and desires. You're also free to express your individuality with art on your boomerangs, and by trying new throws, catches and games."

✦ John Flynn
White River Junction, Vermont

AKA Fast Flynn

"Boomerangs are always a challenge, because boomerang throwing is never perfect. It is a never ending chance to improve, both in trying out new technology and in exercising your creative side, making new boomerangs."

John Flynn – 1995
USA Nationals Champion

John bought his first boomerang when he was a freshman in college. He threw it into a tree, losing both his boomerang and his interest in throwing one.

But not, fortunately, forever. Five years later, he got a job at a windmill company, where he met co-worker and boomerang legend Eric Darnell. After a boomerang get together at Eric's house, John started tossing again. It was sure a good thing that he did.

In 1981, early in John's second-go-round in boomerang throwing, he decided to make his own MTA boom. "I threw it, then I had to duck," he said, "because it came back so fast." John said he didn't yet know anything about tuning a boomerang, so he wasn't aware that his boomerang was turned downwards, where an MTA is always turned upwards.

Okay, so a pessimist would believe he had just made an incredibly bad MTA boomerang. An optimist, however, would see the possibilities in this low flying, speedy boom. Luckily, John was an optimist. After visiting co-worker Eric Darnell, he noticed Eric working on a boom that was hollowed out underneath. Darnell was improving on the fast catch boom. This was the first time John had ever heard of the fast catch event; it wouldn't however, be the last.

"Normally, the fast catch boomerangs sailed up, and then flew down to the thrower," John said, "much like a boom on a sliding board." At that time, the best throwers could toss and catch a fast catch boom in four seconds," John explained. "After I incorporated Eric's hollowing-out in my warped down boomerang, I had a boomerang that flew low to the ground, going out twenty meters and back in three seconds, and the sport of Fast Catch was forever changed."

Now, it's 1982. The world record for the fast catch - that is, the event where you throw the same boomerang out twenty meters and back five times - was 33 seconds. "Here I was, a 23 year old, new to the sport," John recalled. "I told people at the tournament that I threw the fast catch at home in 24 seconds. I'm not sure anyone believed me."

The first time he competed in fast catch, he would have broken the 33 second world record, tossing at 30 seconds, but he dropped a boom, so officially the time didn't count. Later that summer, however, at the University of Massachusetts, John came back with a vengeance. "I put it all together in competition," John acknowledged.

And that he did - smashing the fast catch event at 26.8 seconds, absolutely shattering the notion that the fast catch record couldn't go below 30 seconds. Score a world record for the new guy!

Not content to rest on his boom accomplishments, however, John scorched the fast catch the next year at 23.7 seconds and the next year again, at 21.8 seconds. Suddenly, the event that couldn't be taken in less than 30 seconds hovered at the 20 second mark. And, you guessed it - the next year, in 1985, John Flynn muscled his way through the 20 second barrier, setting an amazing new world fast catch record of 18.74 seconds. John held the fast catch world record for seven years, and still to this day, no one has ever duplicated his awesome speed with a two-bladed boomerang.

He competed on the United States International Team in 1984, 1987, 1988, 1989 and 1991, serving as co-captain of the winning team in 1991 and 1994. "I skipped the 1992 competition because of a broken foot," John said, "and the 1996 tournament because of work and family commitments."

Although the Americans lost in 1984, John was a vital part of the winning team in 1989, as well as those in 1991 and 1994. The only reason his team lost in 1987 and 1988 is because they were beaten out by another American team. And, when Chet Snouffer e-mailed his United States colleagues from New Zealand, announcing the 1996 German win over the United States, Chet's first comment shows how vital a team player John really is.

"We won the first day, then Mike Dickson got hurt and the German *Young Guns* pulled ahead by 5 points on the second day," Chet wrote. "Without Mike, and without Rob (Parkins) and John Flynn, we just didn't quite have the firepower we needed."

"I count on my experience during my boomerang throwing," John said. "Experience is important, but I'm still learning. I'll always keep learning more about boomerangs."

"Americans grow up throwing baseballs and footballs, developing a natural overhand throwing motion," he said. "We love the big outdoors and the open spaces, as well." He also points out the American competitive spirit. "We figure out how to win, even with teams made up of people from very different backgrounds," he said. "There are so many intangibles in this sport."

Ranked number 2 overall in the United States in 1995, John easily snagged the US National Championships, clinching the title before the final event even took place. He also tied the then United States accuracy record, earning 48 out of 50 points in that precision throwing event. More than thirteen years after John set his first world record, he still commands enormous respect on the throwing field.

Since 1994, he has been able to intertwine his work and his love of boomerangs into one. John earned the enviable job of the Product and Marketing Manager of the Toys That Fly and Recreational Sport Boomerang Division of Safesport Outdoor Gear. One of the products that John sells is the boomerang line designed by former co-worker, Eric Darnell.

Besides selling boomerangs and throwing boomerangs, John is also a boomerang craftsman, his natural elbow boomerangs earning him a 1994 craftsmanship award. "In what other sport can you get enjoyment out of making your equipment and then more enjoyment in using it?" John asked, answering his own question. "No other sport. None."

✦ Michael Girvin

Berkeley, California

AKA Michael Gel Girvin
AKA Gel

> *"The definition of Team Gel: You go out and give 150 percent effort and try, and try, and try so hard that you're defining what fun is!"*

Team Gel took the 1985 US National Boomerang Tournament by storm. "We hand painted all our own jerseys and brightly decorated all our boomerangs with rad art, and we gave 150 percent effort," Michael said. "Of course, we were all just beginners, and we didn't do well in the boomerang events."

Michael and Moleman, another new thrower, had recently started a California based boomerang club, *Team Gel*. After finding out that the Nationals were to be held in Los Angeles, they signed their team up. "We were enthusiastic to go and throw, and give it our best shot," Michael said.

"We didn't know how to do many of the tournament events at all," Michael said. "Moleman practiced and practiced the juggling event, and then, in the tournament, he got a zero."

Michael "Gel" Girvin
Five-time World record holder

Moleman did a backflip on the field anyway. "Our team attitude was that we'd have a great time, regardless if we won or lost," Michael said.

But Team Gel? "Gel has two meanings," Michael said. "One is the literal meaning, that of coming together. In skateboarding, however, to gel is to fall apart, to do a terrible job." He added, "By combining those two meanings, we came up with our team name." About the team's first tournament, he enthused, "In the process of trying every event, even though we got some zeroes, we learned a great deal. We gelled in both the literal meaning of the word, and the skateboarding slang sense. The two meanings of the word "gel" simultaneously existed, and this brought us together as a Team!"

Michael Gel Girvin is an amazing all around kind of guy, moving on from the 1985 US Nationals to his own place in the sun. A five-time world record holder, he was selected for the United States International Team in every year from 1987 to 1994. Boomerang artist Dr. Fredric Malmberg describes Michael as having the most fluid throwing motion of anyone around, and Malmberg recommends beginners watch Michael throw.

The 1989 World Champion of Fast Catch, and the Most Valuable Player in the 1989 World Championships, Michael is also a nationally recognized boomerang artist, formally trained at the Chicago Institute of Art. Receiving three national awards for best boomerang decoration, three for the most original boomerang design and two others for technological advance, his boomerangs have been used by seven different champions, while they set eleven world records. He owns and operates his own boomerang business, Gel Boomerangs.

Note: Hinged box with boom poem inside   *Note: Central Beads spell "BOOM"*

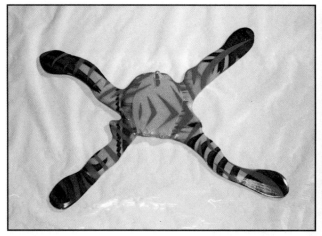 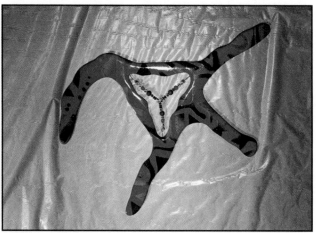

*Gel Art
Boomerangs
Whimsical designs by
Michael Gel Girvin*

"I've created boomerangs over the years, using unique shapes and flights," he said. "The art and decoration and color of the boomerangs are as important to me as the air foils built into them for flight." Gel's more ornate artistic boomerangs include beading, and hinged boxes that may contain Gel's own poetry. "I describe the boomerang, and then I put the poem in the box," he said.

"I've tried to do a little of everything in the boomerang world, " he added, "from the making of boomerangs to the art to the exciting competitive side. I also enjoy teaching people how to throw boomerangs."

Girvin has sponsored more than eighty boomerang tournaments, some for the USBA, others for Team Gel and the Bay Area Boomerang Club. While he uses the same basic format for each of the tournaments, only the USBA sanctioned events count towards season ratings.

For the past twelve years, he has also held weekly, three hour long boomerang teaching sessions, open to the public at no cost. "I use the Team Gel philosophy of being positive instead of intimidating, and that gets people interested, and brings them back."

"Whenever Michael is throwing in the park, people surround him, " said world class thrower Doug DuFresne. "He brings in people with his positive energy and general radness. I can't imagine what the west coast would be like without his influence." Michael's boom students range from six year old kids to people in their seventies, with ten to forty people showing up each week, depending on the weather.

"I did this while I attended school in Chicago, too, and we threw in snow storms and huge winds. It was brutal weather," Michael said. "Then, when I held them in Olympia Washington, we had one year that was so rainy that my boomerang posters offered boomerang lessons, come *rain* or *rain*."

Here's a testimony from one of Gel's former students, the man who recently finished in second place in the world individual tournaments in New Zealand. "I owe Gel everything," said world class American thrower Steve Kavanaugh. "He's the person I ask about boomerangs. He infused energy into boomerangs when interest was dwindling. He gives so much to the sport, including his incredible art."

Since Michael did not travel to New Zealand this year, after having surgery, Steve Kavanaugh helped hand out the yearly *Gel Awards*. "Every time I have a tournament, we hand out awards to every thrower, not just people in first, second or third place," Michael said. "If I have fifty people compete in one of my tournaments, I hand out fifty awards."

Since 1987, he has also compiled a list of every competitor, judge, family member and local politician attending the world tournaments, creating a special award for each. "The first year we did the *Team Gel Awards*, people were amazed that everyone received an award," Michael said. "They were overjoyed." The judges in the 1994 World Tournament held in Japan were especially delighted, according to Michael. And, in 1996, the victorious German Young Guns boomerang team was comprised entirely of throwers who adhered to the Gel philosophy. "They're hard core Gellers," Michael said.

Another boom trend, that of **GLORP** (a game similar to HORSE in basketball) can be traced back to Michael's enthusiasm. A local California band named Project Six wrote a song about the planet GLORP, a place where there are no cars or airplanes; instead, the alien creatures ride on boomerangs.

GLORP

"It's the event with the most freedom, really cutting edge," he said. "This event has a rhythm, it's spontaneous. You watch someone try a catch, then someone else tries it. You pull catches that you never have done before. You don't know what you can do until you try it."

People in the Bay Area then created a game named GLORP, with Michael becoming a star GLORP-er. "It's a true freestyle event, with no defined catches," Michael said. "You can be fully creative, maybe bumping a boomerang with your fist, then your head, then catching it after a 360 degree turn."

GLORP is a perfect match for Michael's throwing style and attitude. "I'll even get rad when doing a standard event in a tournament," he said, "maybe catching under the leg when a trick catch is not required. I have more fun that way!"

While Michael sees boomerangs as a hobby, a sport and an art, he has a much larger vision of their worth. "Boomerangs are the perfect metaphor for life," Michael said, "because whatever you throw out comes back to you. Throw booms. Get rad. Have fun."

He sees the metaphor this way: "Whatever boomerang you throw comes back to you, and whatever you do in life comes back to you, as well. However you treat someone, that's how you'll be treated. Boomerangs are a metaphor for both life and love."

And, here's a final thought about boomerangs from Michael Gel:

"Boomerang throwing is fun and beauty and unabashed intelligence."

✦ John Gorski
Avon, Ohio

AKA "Air Gorski"

It was August 8, 1993. The place, Delaware, Ohio.

The boomerang soared into the summer sky. John shielded his eyes from the glaring sun, staring at his boomerang dotting the air in the midst of clouds.

Competing in a spontaneous maximum time aloft event, he hoped the boom would float as long as possible. The previous record for a boomerang staying in the air, then being caught by the thrower, was 2 minutes and 59 seconds.

"After about 30 to 60 seconds, it was obvious that the boomerang got caught in a thermal," said Chet Snouffer. "Then, it drifted slowly to the north, at least 200 meters in the sky." John's boomerang graced the sky for far more than the three minutes he'd hoped for. Around the ten minute mark, the boomerang slid across to hang over the Olentangy River. John shed his shoes, planning to swim across the river, if necessary. If he didn't catch the descending stick, the throw didn't count.

Suddenly, the boomerang changed directions, and it started to descend about 30 meters from the original throwing spot. John jumped up, following the rang to a soccer field, where it spun over a soccer game. John and fellow boomerangers begged the officials to stop the game, pointing to the falling stick.

"I knew this was going to be the most important catch of my life," he said. "I knew I had to grab it."

In front of a crowd of hundreds of people, about 50 meters from the spot where John tossed the rang, he snatched the falling boomerang, after an astonishing flight of 17 minutes, 6 seconds!

One... two... three... four... five... six.........hey, that's one thousand and twenty six seconds long! "John could have thrown his boomerang, driven to McDonald's, eaten lunch and gotten back in time to catch it," Gary Broadbent said, as an observer, time keeper and cheerleader to the amazing throw.

John was a fairly new thrower in the boomerang world when he tossed his extraordinary throw. After participating in a tough com-

John "Air" Gorski
"The Man Who Threw the Boom Heard 'Round the World."

petition the day before, several of the top throwers decided to throw again the following day. And, the rest is history, as word of John's amazing throw spread to rang enthusiasts across the continents. John had just tossed the boom that was heard around the world.

"John has an incredible arm, and he can pump an MTA like nobody's business," said Steve Kavanaugh. "He's going to only get better, as he lives up to his potential."

Soon after that throw, John said his goal was to make the American team for the 1996 New Zealand competition. And, he succeeded. "It was weird to go there and have so many people come up to me and say — Oh! You're the one with the seventeen minute throw!"

After ranking 22nd in the world cup in New Zealand, John expects 1997 to be a great throwing year for him. "Now that I've been on the US team, I'm much more confident," he said. "It was a great learning experience; if you didn't go, you missed out on the new technology, and you might start the season at a disadvantage."

While John is definitely competitive, he said that he throws for the love of the flight of the boomerang. "When you're at a tournament, though, you don't even have to mention any of that," he said. "Everyone there has fallen in love with boomerangs, or they wouldn't have showed up."

He hopes boomeranging will become a sport like beach volleyball; not a huge one, but one with spectator interest. "We need media coverage, with people throwing and watching boomerangs on Sundays like they do with golf," he said. "To do that, though, we may need a different, more exciting format at our tournaments."

John practices two hours a day, four days a week during the boomerang season of April through October. "Still, there is something fascinating, almost mystical about boomerangs," he said. "it represents science, the arts and history, and maybe that's why it sparks interest in people."

"I'm still amazed at how boomerangs work," he added. "Throwing is a different experience each time, with the boomerangs flying in different directions, in various patterns. I'm absolutely in awe of the MTA, as it flies up and then gently floats down."

The sport, according to John, is on its way up. "It's going to grab the attention of people sooner or later," he said. "I expect it to become bigger, thanks to the efforts of people like Gary Broadbent who take boomerangs into the schools. Kids will grow up loving boomerangs."

✦ Steve Kavanaugh

Seattle, Washington

"A boomerang has poetic beauty. It's an inanimate object that comes to life as you throw it. Your boomerang is like a friend you know so well that you know their thoughts even before they speak them."

Steve started tossing boomerangs while attending Evergreen State College in Olympia, Washington. He couldn't even catch a boom until his second or third time out, however, and he performed "mediocre-ly well" in his first tournament in 1987.

A guy like that probably shouldn't seriously pursue competitive throwing, right? Mark that *wrong* with a capital W. In 1996 Steve competed on *USA Team 2* in New Zealand, helping that team finish third in the world. Besides that, he placed second in the world in the individual tournaments, the highest placing of any American in the 1996 World Cup.

And, even more than that, he finished first in the two *Head 2 Head* competitions that he competed in. Head 2 Head? Yes, just when you think you've got this offbeat sport all figured out, someone tosses you a curve.

Competitive throwers have wrestled with the fairness of tournaments in the face of variable winds. Consider this: thrower A tosses in an event, in pleasant wind conditions, and the thrower scores well. Five minutes later, equally talented thrower B steps into the throwers' circle, but a vicious wind has kicked up. Who do you think would do better in the tournament?

Steve Kavanaugh
Took 2nd Place in
1996 World Cup Individuals

To help correct this imbalance, Gregg Snouffer and other throwers have devised head-to-head competitions, where two throwers toss at the same time, in different areas of the field. Whoever scores higher moves on. As far back as 1976, Eric Darnell had experimented with a competition style called Position, which is echoed in the new *Head 2 Head*.

Well, in the New Zealand competitions, the top eight scorers in each individual event competed in a head to head in their successful event. Steve competed in the trick catch category and the MTA, snagging a first place for each. "The New Zealand individuals competition was, no doubt, my proudest accomplishment with boomerangs," Steve said.

In an ironic twist, while this was Steve's second international competition on an American team, he has actually competed internationally four times. He first competed in the world tournament in 1989, when it was held in Washington DC. "It was a great experience, meeting other throwers, getting further exposed to the sport," he said. "I hadn't even competed in my first nationals yet."

In 1991, he headed to Australia, to watch the action. While he wasn't competing on the United States team, he planned to toss in the individual events. An Australian team needed an extra player, however, so he willingly obliged. "This is a common occurrence, when a team needs an extra player," Steve said.

There, he won the Aussie Round for individuals, his first world-class throwing accomplishment. In 1992, Steve repeated his strategy, flying to Germany to compete in the world individuals. "This time, I threw for the Italian team," Steve said, with a laugh, "the third country I'd thrown for."

Then, in 1996, Steve was chosen to throw for the United States, earning his place in USBA folklore. "While I hoped the Americans would win the team event, I think the German win added hunger to the sport."

He credits Michael Gel Girvin for introducing him to the fascinating sport. Steve practiced throwing on Friday afternoons in a club Gel created. "Michael stressed going out and having fun, about having positive thoughts," Steve said.

Michael returns the compliment. "Steve is absolutely unparalleled as a guy who always has fun when he throws," Michael said. "His unabashed strength is that he always has a smile on his face, and that is conducive to being able to throw under any context. Not everyone can do that. Steve is definitely one of the best freestylers in the world, a real free-spirited and creative thrower."

✦ Bob Leifeld

Chicago, Illinois

AKA Chicago Bob

Bob absolutely couldn't believe it. His college friend Jacques was actually claiming that he went to a boomerang tournament where people travelled to America from France and Germany to compete.

"Jacques was telling me about an International Team Cup that he had participated in," Bob said. "A friend and I finally decided to drive to Delaware, Ohio, where a boomerang tournament was supposed to be held the next day." Travelling through the night, they arrived in the small Ohio town at 4 a.m., sleeping the rest of the night on picnic tables in the park.

"When I woke up, there were all these boomerang throwers," Bob said, "but there were only seven people signed up for the novice category, so they signed me up, even though I'd hardly ever even thrown a boomerang before." He was a little nervous about competing. "My first successful throws - by those, I mean ones that came back anywhere near me," Chi Bob said, "were during that novice tournament."

And, successful throws they were. Bob placed second in the 1987 novice event, and snagged the MTA title in his division. "Since I kept bragging about how far we'd driven to compete, and since I never gave them my last name, Chet Snouffer listed my second place win under the name Chicago Bob, and the nickname stuck."

"I felt foolish later on, though, when I found out people had travelled from all over the country to compete there."

Then, by the time the 1988 Nationals rolled around, people welcomed Bob. "Lots of people came up to me," he said, "and they said - Oh, so you're Chicago Bob!"

Chi's reputation in the boom world firmly in place, Chet Snouffer asked Bob to compete on a team of the best Midwest throwers. He agreed, and the team won nine out of twelve events during the 1991 United States National Team Championships.

That year was a good one for Chicago Bob, as he then won the National Doubling title in the Individual competitions during the same tournament, right in Bob's lucky spot of Delaware, Ohio. Then, in 1995, Bob won the Aussie Round in Minneapolis at the US Open.

*Chicago Bob Leifeld
Member of USA Team 2
at New Zealand*

A member of Team 2 in the 1996 world championships in New Zealand, he helped his team take 3rd place among all the top-ranked teams in the world. (USA teams finished 2nd and 3rd, behind the German Young Guns in the nine-country competition.) Here are some of his impressions from that world class competition. "It was an amazing experience, and the whole ambiance both on and off the field was great," he said. "You could just walk up to any team, anywhere, and have a great conversation. It was nice to finally put faces to all the names I've heard about for so many years."

Bob was also impressed with the organization of the American teams. "Gregg Snouffer yelled constant updates on the MTA throws, and those kind of little things definitely helped." The Americans also had a warm-up jog and a team stretch before throwing.

"Other teams saw this and some did it, too, but we seemed the only ones who did it seriously. And, it helped a lot. We threw, including practice, 10 out of 11 days, and I never got very sore, thanks to the stretching."

Chi-Bob was happy with his personal performance in the team events. "My goal was to do my part, and not mess anything up," he said. He succeeded. "I had a couple little mishaps, neither of which hurt the team much, if at all. Our team operated well, and we didn't drop much." Bob said the tournament reinforced the importance of boom fundamentals. "The saying is old as dirt," he said, "but if you catch, you win."

And, while Bob will never forget the camaraderie and excitement of the New Zealand trip, a simpler, more poetic boomerang moment still lingers in his mind: He had decided to take a trip with friends to Mount Shasta in Northern California. The 14,162 foot mountain towers over surrounding peaks, ones that rise a mere 4 to 5 thousand feet, according to Chi Bob.

Standing in Panther's Meadow, he tossed a bright red boom around Shasta, the mountain said to have mystical powers. "Even though we were standing at 8000 feet altitude, that boom had to have risen more than 6000 feet," Bob said. The boomerang, as though a form of pure and free thought itself, climbed to the top of the mountain. It kept going up and up, until it flew right up and over it, the disappearing flashes of red contrasting against Shasta's snow-capped peak. Then, it vanished, never to be seen again. "It was awesome," Bob recalls, "just awesome."

✦ The Moleman

Shelton, Connecticut

Hardly ever, ever known as John Anthony.

Hmm ...the Moleman ... hey, haven't we heard that name somewhere before? Wasn't he the guy who scored a zero in the national boomerang tournament held in California? Wasn't he the man with the absolute nerve to turn a backflip after that miserable performance?

And, if so, what does he have to say for himself? "Actually, I think I may have scored a zero in both fast catch and juggling," Moleman admits, with a laugh. "Or maybe I caught one boomerang while juggling."

So, after that humble beginning, he certainly couldn't have done well in the boom world, could he? He probably tucked away all his unsnared boomerangs, and crawled away, desperately trying to forget all about his 1985 performance. Now, lots and lots of people might do that. It would be very tempting to do that. But there is one person in the world who absolutely, positively would not do that, and that is the Moleman.

"I was working a dinky little job when the national tournament came to LA, and I spent every last bit of money to get there, so I decided I was just going to have a good time, and enjoy the beach. I think Team Gel members shocked everyone with our wild hairdos and crazy outfits, but we were just excited to be there."

Soon after his exhilarating experience at the nationals, the Moleman moved to the East Coast.
"Then, I saw there was a boomerang display at the Peabody Museum at Yale University, and I went," Moleman said. "I saw Ben and Barnaby Ruhe there, and Peter and Larry Ruhf. They thought I'd come all the way from California for the display."

After Moleman had thrown for a couple of years, he visited Larry Ruhf's house, where he saw Larry's ten year old son, Adam, tossing the fast catch in just 25 seconds. "I was about twenty seven then, and I could only do the fast catch in 30 seconds," he said. "There was no way I wanted a ten-year old to beat me, so I started practicing."

Now, if practice doesn't exactly make perfect, the Moleman proves that it helps. A lot. He began earning first places in various events, including setting the official national MTA limited record at

*John Anthony "Moleman"
Aussie Round World Record
Holder*

one minute, nineteen seconds. Since the early days of the unlimited maximum time aloft, a restriction has been placed on the event. Now, in MTA limited, AKA *MTA-100*, the thrower must catch the boomerang within 100 meters of the original throwing spot, in order for the throw to count.

"One minute and nineteen seconds is only five seconds off the world record," he said. "My boomerang had actually headed in the opposite direction from where it should have, rising over the trees. As it started falling, people were yelling and screaming that it would be a record, so I'm really glad I caught it."

In 1995, he also set the Aussie Round world record in a competition held in Hartford, Connecticut. *Aussie Round*, explained further later in this book, is an awesomely tough event combining throwing skills, accuracy skills and distance skills. And, in an another amazing performance, the Moleman, the very same Moleman who scored a zero in 1985, snagged the 9th place spot in the 1996 World Individual Tournament in New Zealand.

"When I was down to my last throw, I thought I had to get a really good throw to even place in the top twenty," he said. "Then, I had a mediocre toss, and I found out I earned a ninth place finish." The most important thing for Moleman, however, is that he had a good time, while doing his best. "Even if you end up in last place, it doesn't matter as long as you went out and enjoyed your best efforts."

He remembers another tournament in Europe in 1992, when he was in first place, with only one throw remaining. "I'd never gotten a first place in a tournament overall, and all I needed was an average throw to get one," he said. "I didn't throw well at all, though, and I dropped to seventh overall."

He walked away, and sat by himself for ten minutes. "I was getting down on myself," he said. "Then, I thought — hey, here I am in Belgium — I should be having a great time! So, I did."

And, to be on the safe side, the Moleman always carries good luck charms with him on the throwing field, wearing a black fedora between events. "Steve Kavanaugh comes up to me before a tournament, and asks me which boomerang he should use," Moleman said. "I hit myself on the head with one of them, and I say — okay, that looks like the right one."

He remembers one exceptionally special boom moment. "About two years after Team Gel hit the boomerang scene, Ben Ruhe presented us with a big brass cup, calling it the flight of fancy award. He gave a speech about how we'd helped change the boomerang world, adding excitement to the tournaments. That meant more to me than anything else, because before that, I figured that other throwers only thought we were strange."

Moleman puts on demonstrations at schools and Boy Scout events, until recently bringing along his boomerang-catching pit bull, the *Gel Dog*. "We made her our team mascot, since she instinctively started catching boomerangs when she was about three months old," he said. After catching a boomerang during a demo, *Gel Dog* always trotted out a victory circle before returning the boom to her master. "She still chases the boomerang around in a circle, though," Moleman said. "She hasn't yet figured out that she can sit and wait for the boomerang to return to her."

While *Gel Dog* will probably never figure that principle out, Michael Gel Girvin gladly explains the Moleman to us. "Moleman has absolutely the biggest heart in the boomerang world," said Michael. "He's one of those throwers who does everything well, and he's solid in team competition. While a problem may seem insurmountable to most people, it won't seem that way to Moleman. He sees the good in everything, and that's reflected in his throwing and in his life."

✦ Barnaby Ruhe
Emmaus, Pennsylvania

After Barnaby competed on the Masters Team in the 1996 World Championships in New Zealand, he'd hoped for a chance to swim with the dolphins. Unfortunately, that didn't work out, and Barnaby was disappointed, to say the least.

"Suddenly, though, I realized I had already been swimming with the dolphins," Barnaby said. "I'd just spent days with the most absolutely inventive people, who had been flipping on the wind layers, skidding, screaming and flying, having the greatest time. We'd been in the spirit of the dolphins, moment by moment, like being drenched by a dolphin avalanche."

Barnaby Ruhe is certainly an original thinker, and that has served him well in the slightly eccentric, extremely imaginative sport of boomeranging. A former classmate of Oliver North's at the Naval Academy, he has earned both a B.S. in Engineering, as well as a PhD in Shamanism and Modern Painting.

He started throwing boomerangs at his Uncle Ben Ruhe's workshop at the Smithsonian Institute in 1976. "About 2000 people showed up," he said. "Boomerangs just struck a fanciful nerve."

"It didn't occur to any of us to make boomerangs look like just another typical sport," he added. "It was really a stone-aged ritual launched into the space age, skipping over the machine age entirely. As a slightly illogical person, then, I thought if we weren't going to make it look like other sports, then we should go completely in the opposite direction."

Barnaby said his uncle asked him to help create rules for boomerang competitions. "I tried to ignore the social rules of sports, those that existed long before this," he said. "That is why you see women competing side by side with the men in boomerang tournaments."

Early on, Ben and Barnaby and his cousin Peter Ruhf were reading frisbee rules, when they saw an event where the frisbee was to stay in the air as long as possible. "The frisbee only stayed in the air for about ten seconds," he said, "and we thought - hey, boomerangs have wings! Let's use that event. I also starting realizing that all sports have a certain ethos or spirit that we needed to concentrate on."

Barnaby Ruhe
Pioneer Tournament Rulesmaker

Barnaby compares the integration of freestyle boomerang throwing techniques into tournament action with the Harlem Globetrotters and their brand of basketball. "While the Globetrotters passed the ball backwards, and between their legs, it was all in fun," he said. "Eventually, however, basketball players have incorporated this into real competition. They've integrated serious basketball play with show time, creating an unabashed good time."

Barnaby first created the boomerang foot catch with this theory in mind. "We had to become more risky, a little more silly," he said, "and as long as you incorporated that into the rules, it became okay. Now, the foot catch is in the international rules."

He believes the sport took another giant leap when Michael Gel Girvin and his gang entered the fray. "He was radically a screwball, shaking with jello," he said. "He was with an unruly bunch of skateboarders, and when they showed up, the sport changed further into the direction I'd hoped for."

It may sound like Barnaby has spent his time observing other throwers, while reading and writing boomerang rules. That, however, is far from the case. He has competed, he is still competing and he always competes as hard as he can. His first dramatic win was during the 1978 Nationals, held in Washington DC. "I'd recently run a marathon, so I was in the better shape of my life," he said, "but the contest was still dead even until the last event, so we decided to have a suicide tie breaker."

In *Suicide*, two or more throwers continually toss boomerangs, with throwers out of the contest when they drop a boom. While many throwers, for safety reasons, are glad that suicide is not a regular tournament event, Barnaby disagrees. "The glory of two hundred throwers tossing simultaneously attracts photographers like a bevy of quails," he said. "It's definitely fireworks."

He also likes the suicide philosophy of all or nothing throwing. "It's too abstract for me when you say nine out of ten catches is good," he said. "That's a hard concept to grasp, but I can say I won fifty percent of the suicides for about ten years. I ruled."

Let's go back to the 1978 Nationals. At the end of the *Suicide* toss-off, no winner had been decided. So, Barnaby and his opponent went one step further, and (drum roll please!), they played *Mayhem*.

Each competitor had to throw one boomerang, and to win the Nationals title, the thrower had to catch both boomerangs. Barnaby tossed his rang out a short distance, caught it, and then had time to catch the other competitor's magnificently thrown rang.

"I ran full speed towards the other boomerang, and towards the other thrower, and I flew chest high into the air, cleats first," he said. "It was definitely a concluding moment."

Barnaby also noted a large number of Frenchmen defecting from skateboarding to boomerang tossing around that same time. "The French are lots of fun," he added.

He believes the sport needs more defining moments like that. "We need single moments, home run moments when we see who is the hero," he said. "We've had those many times in the past."

Barnaby also won the 1986 Nationals, and he has competed on several international teams. Appearing on *That's Incredible* in 1982, and with Jay Leno on the *Tonight Show* in 1994, he estimates that he has been seen throwing by 65 million people.

"Once, this little kid in France starts beating me in boomerangs," he said, "and I find out he saw me on television *five years earlier.*"

While Barnaby longs for those individual, gloriously peaking moments, he praises team efforts, as well. He credits his cousin Larry Ruhf for the progression of the team events. "Sports return to their joyous nature in teams," he said, "because you get a little wilder, in and out of a circle, back to the place it can be."

He also acknowledges yet another group of throwers. "Nine tenths of boomerangs throwers," he said, "are throwing and catching during the magical dawn, for the sheer enjoyment of it. You'll never meet them at a tournament. And that's okay. People just have a primal urge to throw boomerangs."

✦ Adam Ruhf

Belchertown, Massachusetts

AKA Baby Boomer

Chet Snouffer grew up admiring the boom skills of the Ruhe/Ruhf clan, including Larry Ruhf, a member of the first U.S. team to compete internationally. Then, Larry's son Adam grew up watching Chet Snouffer, in awe of Chet's powerfully athletic feats. Now that Chet Snouffer's young son is learning about boomerangs, who is he watching?

Adam Ruhf! Just like the sport, the names and faces in the boom world keep going round and round in circles, mimicking the graceful curve of the magical stick itself.

Adam Ruhf is the youngest thrower to ever make the United States international team. In 1995, at the age of 15, Adam was the national runner-up behind John Flynn. In the same amazing year, he set the United States fast catch record, snagging five booms in just 16.5 seconds, and he spent the month of July as the top ranked American thrower.

"Adam is a phenomenal athlete," the Moleman said. "He's got the mental awareness, along with incredible athletic ability. I think this will take him all the way to the top."

After he set the American record for *fast catch*, Adam described his ultimate boom goal - to smash the seemingly out of reach world *fast catch* record of just 15.03 seconds, held by Gregory Biseaux of France since 1991. In 1996 the record was Adam's.

Chosen the October 1995 *Sports Illustrated* Old Spice Athlete of the Month, Adam travelled to New Zealand, serving America on *Team 1*. Although reports have said that Adam won the Old Spice award before he started shaving, he vehemently denies that rumor.

Adam Ruhf Co-holder of World Endurance Throw Record & World record holder in Fast Catch

This, however, is an undisputed fact: Adam first started tossing a rang at the age of eighteen months, beginning competition play at age eight. One bystander recalls watching eight-year old Adam throw and catch five boomerangs in just 25 seconds, commenting that the boomerang was half the size of Adam himself.

By the age of ten, Adam had beaten his athletic, record-setting father in competition. When 13, he already ranked 15th in the nation, and he was voted the 1995 *Many Happy Returns* MHR Boomeranger of the Year.

The choice for the MHR boomeranger was tough. Chet Snouffer came back in 1995 to sweep the ratings, and John Flynn snagged the nationals. Moleman set a new world record, and Betsy Miale-Gix held onto the fast catch record for half of the season. Chicago Bob and John Gorski each won their first USBA tournament, and Norm Kern won the Open Class at the U.S. Open. But, here's what the USBA had to say about Adam.

"This young star had developed the instinct to track a boom in flight. He had learned the subtleties of the humpback throw; knew the intricacies of weighting for drag and wind; and perhaps most difficult of all, had developed that most illusive of all competitive traits: an appeal. As screaming boom groupies lined fields from Massachusetts to Minnesota in order to catch a glimpse of the charismatic chucker, the affable youngster rarely hesitated to deliver."

*"And, so with his sails set and his sights on New Zealand, 15 year old Adam Ruhf enters a brave new age of Boomerang History as MHR's **1995 Boomstud of the Year.**"*

> *While Adam learned plenty about different wind conditions in the tournaments, he learned one far more important lesson. "I hurt my throwing abilities when I get mad at myself," he said. "I've learned not to let a mistake get me down - you just have to go on."*

Adam loved his 1996 New Zealand adventure, ending up with a ranking of 13th in the world in individual events. "People who hadn't heard about my competing there were surprised to see someone so young," he said. "I was just two throws away from getting fourth in the world, and only a couple more than that from a first place finish."

He was amazed at the new MTA technology he saw Axel Heckner use in the team events. "He had a three bladed MTA, and I've got one of the only other two that exist. It was fantastic, and I expect to see them cropping up in the Nationals."

He compares and contrasts the different throwing styles around the world. "I found the Americans and Germans to have similar styles, while the Swiss threw harder, and the Australians used more finesse. The French take plenty of chances, and they never take the safe route."

Adam admits that he dislikes the conservative style of throwing that is rewarded by the international scoring system. "The American style of scoring rewards throwers who take chances, while the scoring system used throughout Europe rewards safer, more conservative styles. You often do better by being consistently mediocre."

It's unlikely, however, that Adam Ruhf will ever back off from his take charge throwing style. Instead of taking it easy after his international throwing stint, for example, he came back to work even harder. On June 14, 1996, he was practicing for a competition that would be held in his home state of Massachusetts the next day. "I broke the fast catch world record three times that day in practice," Adam said, "one time at 14.30 and two times at 14.40. That put it in my mind that I could set a new world record the next day."

To be on the safe side, Adam wore the exact same clothing to the tournament that he wore during practice, down to the same pair of lucky socks. He wrote his girlfriend's name on the shoulder of his undershirt, and right before he was to compete in the fast catch competition, he put on a special crocheted skull cap. "My uncle had given me that hat, and I decided it would be my lucky hat," Adam said, "but I'd never worn it before that day."

He kissed his shoulder where his girlfriend's name rested, then knelt down and prayed. "I got a 16.69 in the first of my two rounds of fast catch, almost matching my American record," Adam said. "Then, I think I really shocked people when I threw my second round in just 14.98 seconds."

Adam Ruhf, barely 16 years old, had just smashed the fast catch world record, blazing his way to his first world record. But, he isn't ready to rest after his recent accomplishments. For example, in September, 1996, he set another world record: fast catch of 14.60! "Now, I'd like to be the National Champion...," he said, "then set the endurance world record." And, that may well happen. While the endurance world record, held by Yannick Charles of France, stands at 76 catches in five minutes, Adam has already snagged 90 boomerangs in a practice trial of the event. (Editor's note: See World Records and Virginia Beach notes for results of the 1996 Nationals.)

Adam explains why he feels Americans hold so many boomerang records. "Americans win so many international events because they are competitive, yet they still have fun," he said. Adam suspects there will be many more tough eight-hour competition days ahead of him. "Just think, I could throw in national and international competitions for fifteen more years," he said. "And, I'll still only be thirty years old."

Moleman agrees with that sentiment, and he laughs about playing *GLORP* with Adam. "With *GLORP* , you get into a line, with the person with the fewest years of throwing experience going to the head of the line, and the person with the most years ending up at the end," he said. "Here is a teenager, the youngest thrower, standing at the end of the line!"

At present, a straight A high school student, a varsity baseball pitcher and a whiz at math and science, Adam makes and sells boomerangs from home. "I made $1,000 in one summer making competition boomerangs," he said. "I'd like to get into that side of boomerangs more someday." Although fellow students wished him well in New Zealand, many of them didn't realize how talented he was until he started receiving national press attention in 1996. He loves being part of a winning team, calling himself a serious competitor.

And, while he is certainly serious about competition, he also has a reputation as being an all around great guy. Here's how three time world champion Chet Snouffer describes this 16 year-old boomerang star. "He's one of the nicest, most sincere and *fastest* people you will ever meet on the boom circuit."

"A boomerang tournament is a grueling marathon, eight hours of pure competition."

"The sport of boomeranging is a curious sport. It attracts a certain kind of person - very individualistic. You can be older, and the finesse and knowledge count that much more. You don't need brute strength."
(Larry Ruhf, former MTA record holder — and Adam's proud dad.)

✦ *Gregg Snouffer*
Delaware, Ohio

Gregg's description of a boomerang trip to Sedona, Arizona:
" It had been a magic week, one that reaffirmed our belief in the power of a prehistoric tool of unknown origin. Everyone knows of its ability to mysteriously fly out and return to its thrower. But we were aware also of its magical ability to bring strangers together and turn them into friends, to unite those friends from across the country and from around the world."

Gregg Snouffer won the 1991 World Indoor Championship in Perth, Australia.

Powerful words, for sure. But don't expect to meet a super-serious, stone faced kind of guy when you run across Gregg Snouffer. As the editor of the USBA newsletter, **Many Happy Returns**, no one is safe from his good natured sense of humor.

When one subscriber wrote to praise Gregg's editorial efforts, this was his light-hearted reply: "You like me! You really like me! . . . sniff. . ."

When another thrower from Germany lamented the breakage of one of his prized boomerangs during tuning, Gregg sympathized - with the boom. "To die in the maker's hands," Gregg wrote, "a twisted, wretched, grain-crunching death, must be the worst nightmare in every stick's mind."

When yet a third thrower praised the boomerangs of another world class thrower, Gregg asked if the writer was being bribed to write that letter. "In fact," he added, "I bet your name isn't Jason at all . . . it's you, isn't it, Gary?" Of course, Gregg then provided Jason with information on how to contact Gary.

But, besides serving as the wry-humored Secretary of the USBA, Gregg Snouffer is also a true champion, in many more ways than one! Sometimes seeming to be lost in the shadows as the younger brother of world champion Chet Snouffer, Gregg has competed in international competitions, including a spot on the victorious American teams in both 1987 and 1988.

He had a terrific performance in the world cup in Perth, Australia in 1991, snagging the World Indoor Championship title. "I won three out of the four events in both the prelim and the final tourney," Gregg said, "so I was pretty on that day!" He served well on the winning American team that travelled to Japan in 1994, and he also participated on USA Team 2 in New Zealand in 1996.

Gregg is a main force in introducing a newer, exciting boomerang tournament format, *Head 2 Head*, featured at three American tournaments in 1995, and used during the 1996 New Zealand world cup. To win this format, you need to go through five elimination rounds, so one fantastic round can't snag a title. Each round, you compete against one person who made it to that round by beating someone else, so each round becomes more difficult. To win an event, you need consistently excellent throwing skills.

Head 2 Head adds excitement to the sport, as you're actually tossing at the same time your opponent is, while in traditional tournaments, one thrower tosses at a time. The action is jammed packed, so the tournaments are shorter, yet more dramatic. While traditional tournaments will continue to occur, you can look for more Head 2 Heads in the future.

But, more important than the *Head 2 Head* competitions, and even more important than Gregg's world class throwing skills, is his other style of success. In 1991 , he and brother Chet were both in an extremely close contention for the national title. If Chet did not do well on his last throw of the competition, Gregg would be honored as the highest ranked thrower in the country.

Gregg Snouffer and Mark Weary at Boom Bell Rock, Sedona, Arizona.

Chet made a great final throw, however, and Gregg didn't earn the coveted title. A major disappointment, for sure. So what did Gregg do? He raced over to congratulate and hug his older brother.

Eyewitnesses say Gregg displayed only joy over his brother's win, reminding competitors everywhere of the true purpose of competition. He proved that winners do their personal best in each situation, regardless of whether or not they ever reach the absolute pinnacle of their sport.

But true champions respect other people even more. This asset of Gregg's also plays out in his respect for the planet and all that is in it. Read on about Sedona, a place Gregg describes as "a natural power source."

"In the Sedona area," Gregg writes, "the red rock sandstone is rich in iron, which, they say, amplifies the natural vibrations and electromagnetic energy of mother earth. It is said that the human body in this environment, while resonating at its normal frequency, has a significantly increased amplitude, resulting in a greater feeling of contentment and centeredness. This phenomena has drawn and held settlers to the area since the first people set foot on the North American continent, and possibly before even that."

He, along with Chicago Bob and Mark "Wildman" Weary decided to boom the vortexes in that very place. Writing in words evocative of an almost mystical tone, Gregg explained, "These swirling rivers of electromagnetic energy exist in three forms. The upflows stream up from high places, like mountain tops into the heavens, conveying energy that causes the human spirit to soar. When flowing down from the heavens into earth, they are called downflows, and are places of quiet reflection, such as near the banks of a stream in the bottom of a canyon. The third are horizontal vortexes which are located at overlooks and tend to lend insight into past and future lives."

"If you're familiar with the exalted feeling you have when standing atop a mountain, with the earth at your feet, or the quiet serenity when sitting by a stream, then you have experienced the power of a vortex and the subtle effect that its energy has on your spirit."

In order to toss a boom through all three types of vortexes, the three adventurers hiked and climbed, crossed rivers and ravines. Gregg's description ends with a poetic turn, "Our rangs spiralled out and around dizzying heights, tossed bravely over vistas from which there was no hope of rescue, had our noble booms refused to precess. Our rangs were loyal, however, and we lost not one."

✦ Mark Weary

Phoenix, Arizona

AKA Wildman Weary

"Technical knowledge is not enough. One must transcend techniques so that the art becomes an artless art, growing out of the unconscious."

Mark's performance during the world competitions in New Zealand, 1996, earned him the spot of the third highest ranked boomerang thrower across the planet, and it inspired him to make '96-'97 his best year in competition ever. "My goal is to become the National Champion," he said.

He describes his exciting times in New Zealand. "I just did what I knew I could do," Mark said, "ending the individual portion of the tournament with a perfect *Aussie Round* throw, taking first place in that event. It was a terrific way to finish the competition."

Stepping up to compete in the Head 2 Head competition held after the individual events, Mark snagged a first place Aussie Round finish in that competition, as well. "Success isn't final, though," he added. "You always need to continue working at your throwing skills."

Mark Weary, Zen Boom Master

Mark said that each thrower in New Zealand had a slightly different reason for wanting to be there. "My goal is to always make the United States team, because I want to do something great for my country. I'm driven by that nationalism, and except for one event, I was flawless in the team competition."

Mark believes that a positive attitude towards boomerang throwing brings excellent results. "There are individuals who have thrown twice as long as I have, but they don't do nearly as well. They just expect that others will beat them. I take Michael Jordan's approach to competing, though; I'll never say someone is better than me."

He only started throwing competively about five years ago, so he's a relative newcomer to the sport. Several years ago, however, while working with a guy who owned a little bit of this and a little bit of that, the two co-workers got into a discussion about Australia. "He remembered that he had some boomerangs, but he had lost the instructions, and he'd forgotten how they worked," Mark recalled, with a laugh. "We experimented with them in bad weather conditions in Chicago. Looking back, though, we did pretty well."

Mark then moved from apartment to apartment, packing his magically returning sticks with him each time. "Then, one pristine day, I rediscovered them, and they worked well, so I decided to really get into throwing." Mark ordered boomerangs from the *Boomerang Man*, Rich Harrison, who then put Mark in touch with the USBA. By 1991, Mark was ready to compete in his first tournament. "I was going to go with a friend, but it ended up that he couldn't go," Mark said. "My friend said just to go ahead and look up throwers named Chicago Bob and Reverend Jim, saying they'd take care of me."

And, they did. Mark finished 8th overall in that first tournament, taking a second place spot in doubling. "Boomerang throwers are a real kindred kind of group," he said. "It doesn't matter who you are; you're just accepted. We end up in remote spots all over the world, having a great time together. It must be a previous life kind of thing." That 1991 tournament also sealed Mark's interest in the sport. "I then figured, if I did this well, think how well I could do if I really practiced," Mark said. "So, I set some goals and I improved."

That's certainly an understatement. He set an MTA record of one minute and fifteen seconds; even though that time has been broken, he still has the third best MTA time. Mark set a world record in *Aussie Round* in 1993, and then, after placing second in the nationals a couple of times, he won the national ratings title in 1994.

He was also involved with an amazing coincidence at one tournament. He and fellow thrower Will Gix were tossing the *Aussie Round* event at about the same time. Will finished first, setting an incredible *Aussie Round* world record. "I wasn't really thinking about records, and I just finished my time," Mark said, "and about ten seconds after Will set the world record, I broke it and set my own world record."

While the athletic appeal first drew Mark into the world of boomerangs, he found that the designing of booms quickly grabbed his attention, as well. "I now enjoy the aesthetics of boomerangs, the visual decorating and the beauty aspect of them," he said. Before competing in New Zealand, Mark only made boomerangs for himself and for a few other competitors. He is now considering expanding his boomerang manufacturing, to market sport boomerangs for a larger group. Mark credits four people for helping him get his boomeranging skills in order: Eric Darnell, Doug DuFresne, Barnaby Ruhe and Chet Snouffer.

So, two world records were set at the exact same field, at almost the exact same time!
"It was really cool," Mark said, "but it's a shame that people don't remember the number 2 guy, because Will's throwing was terrific, too."

"Eric knows so much that he can't even remember all he knows," Mark said, with a laugh. "When I was training for an international competition, there were some really weird winds, and Eric bent my boomerang a new way." Eric guaranteed Mark that the boom would fly correctly, and it did. "How come you never told me that before?" Mark asked Eric.

Eric shrugged. "I guess I just re-remembered it."

Mark said Doug DuFresne helped him with his speed, and Barnaby Ruhe aided him with his spiritual approach to boomerangs. Chet Snouffer, of course, helped him with his competitive training techniques.

To keep in top competitive shape, Mark practices martial arts, rides a mountain bike and meditates. "I have a Zen background," he said, "and I get lost in the dance of the boomerang. When I get started throwing, one thing just rolls into another, and I realize aspects of myself that I'd never drawn on before."

Mark uses other aspects of Zen while throwing. "In order to do well at something, you need to have the approach of a child, that of a childlike enthusiasm," he said.

He has a highly unusual practicing technique. He says he throws with his eyes closed. "I can practice better when I do that," he said. "It's interesting, because when you're not looking at what you're doing, then your body feels it. You just keep a picture in your mind, and you can feel the wind." He claims to excel in hitting the accuracy bullseye while practicing this way. "You don't realize how amazing you can throw until you do it with your eyes closed."

He does this during practice rounds of endurance as well. "When you can throw without stopping, you realize how incredible the body is, and how slowly your mind works to acknowledge that."

Anxiety is the enemy of boomerang throwers, according to Mark. "That's when you make mistakes," he said. "You're actually distracting yourself, instead of keeping a oneness. When you can focus, you find how out how you're capable of doing so much more than you'd thought."

Mark offers this advice to those who want to reach the peak of boomerang success. "You just need to lose yourself in the dance, and become a competitor with yourself," he said. "Instead of taking a negative approach towards other competitors, however, you need to always do the best you can personally do. There is no traffic jam on that extra mile, so if you apply yourself, you can accomplish amazing things."

Profile of a Typical Rang-er

Okay, so what's the lesson to be learned from all these sketches of star quality USA and World Champion boom athletes?

Is it:

A) If you can't throw an MTA like John Gorski or perform trick catches like Gary Broadbent, then you should forget about even picking up a boomerang?

B) If you can't snag a boomerang in the middle of a backflip like the talented Snouffer brothers, then you should never, ever toss a boomerang in a public place?

C) If you can't create fast catch miracles like John Flynn or Adam Ruhf, or hit the bullseye like Mark Weary, then you should forget about ever signing up for a boomerang tournament?

The answers to A, B and C are easy - - nope, not at all and no way.

The sport of boomeranging is wide open, with opportunities for males and females, for boys and girls, and for the young and the not-quite-so-young-anymore. Enthusiastic boomerang throwers the world over are a group of highly creative, innovative, "hey — maybe this will work even better— and if it doesn't, what have we really lost?" kind of people. They are the type of people who are willing to continue throwing in unpredictable winds, who tape pennies or snap rubber bands on sticks of curved wood, attempting to adjust the flight of their rang, attempting to perfect the absolutely unperfectable.

Boomerang throwers pose an interesting paradox; while they are a friendly group of people, they also seem to each have a highly individualistic mindset, eager to forge his or her own way in the sport. They are always able to keep alive an incredible spark of enthusiasm for their sport, even when surrounded by personal duties and work responsibilities. They are a generous, welcoming and hospitable group of people, patient with new throwers and eager to share what they know.

And, here's a rather strange coincidence. While just looking at the top ranked American throwers, you'll see two sets of twins; not so strange in itself, but then there are three of the other top rated throwers who have children who are twins. Hmm. . .

On a more scientific note, Ted Bailey conducted a written survey in 1991, collecting data from 100 boomerang throwers, in an attempt to create a profile of a person who is fascinated by the amazing returning stick.

Of those throwers, 96 were male, 3 were female, and 1 preferred not to specify a gender. Seventy-six threw with their right hand, nine with their left, one was ambidextrous and 14 didn't specify. Fifty-one percent were married, thirty-two percent single, five-percent widowed, separated or divorced, with the rest not specifying.

No surprises so far. I found the ages interesting, however, with them ranging from eleven to sixty nine, the average age of a thrower between thirty and forty. One person started throwing at age six, but most started throwing as an adult, with another young at heart individual tossing the first rang at age fifty-five.

One person in the survey had actually been throwing for fifty years, with another close behind with forty-five years experience. Fifty-two throwers had "regular" employment, collecting a paycheck from a boss somewhere, with sixteen throwers self employed. Four combined self employment with a back-up regular job, nine were students, three were retired and three were unemployed.

Okay, now the survey takes off on a lighter, more offbeat note, with Ted discovering a fascinating quirk. Forty-percent of the throwers were born under the signs of Leo, Virgo or Libra, with most of the throwers having birthdays in mid-summer or early winter. Out of only one-hundred throwers, there were five pairs of matching birthdays, four sets under the sign of Leo, with Ted himself involved in a birthday match.

While 18 throwers had no pets, thirty-one had cats, thirty had dogs, three had birds, three had fish, two had gerbils, two had reptiles, two had ants, two had plants, two had crabs and one had slime mold.

As you can see, almost anyone can fit into the boom profile. Do you listen to music? Well, so do boom tossers, with rock and roll being the favorite category for 39 of the throwers. Twenty-four preferred jazz, twenty-two enjoyed classical music, and eight listened to country tunes. Only five relaxed to pop and easy listening tunes, four favored folk and three cried to the blues. Two jammed to reggae, with the following categories each receiving one vote: yoga chanting, ballads, boogie woogie, spiritual, dixieland, tribal, ethnic, eclectic, female vocal, heavy metal, and musical theater.

" You'll certainly now know what music to play after a tournament, " Ted said, in jest.

Okay, the next survey question delved into the languages spoken by the throwers. While two did not reveal the information, one person said he didn't speak English as a first or second language. Forty-five throwers knew more than one language, while nineteen spoke at least three. Twenty of the throwers did not speak English as a primary language, with nine of them speaking French, seven German, two Swedish, one Japanese and one Flemish.

The education of the throwers varied widely, with twenty-three having a high school education, and four obtaining an associates degree. Twenty-nine throwers had a bachelors degree, fifteen earned a masters degree, and four had a Ph.D. There were five doctors in

One person in the survey had actually been throwing for fifty years, with another close behind with forty-five years experience. Fifty-two throwers had "regular" employment, collecting a paycheck from a boss somewhere, with sixteen throwers self employed. Four combined self employment with a back-up regular job, nine were students, three were retired and three were unemployed.

the group, and one thrower with both a Ph.D and an MD.

Curious about the occupations of choice? Seven were involved in computer science and seven were in the medical fields. Six each worked in the arts and physics, and there were five with psychology degrees and five who worked in physical education. Three were involved with biology/chemistry, and there were three anthropologists, as well. The other occupations ranged all over the map, with no other matching occupations.

Now, how many throwers made boomerangs, how large were the throwers' collections and how much did boom enthusiasts spend on their boom purchases annually? Well, out of ninety throwers, sixty-seven made boomerangs, thirty-four of them re-selling some of their handiwork. The average boom manufacturer made one-hundred and seventy-nine boomerangs a year. Eighty-five of the throwers owned 12,268 boomerangs combined, with each individual collection ranging from three to eight hundred boomerangs. The average collection totalled one hundred and forty four.

Eighty-two throwers spent $16,357 on booms in 1990, with the average person spending $200. Out of 87 throwers, three refused to spend more than $10 for a boom, with others spending as much as $250, $300 and $450 for a single boomerang. The average boom purchase totalled $54.

Then, there are the t-shirts. Out of eighty-seven respondents, seventy of them owned an average of 9.5 shirts each, with the biggest shirt owner proudly hanging seventy of them in the closet. Seventeen throwers did not indicate (or own up to) any boom t-shirt purchases at all.

Well, anyhow, the point is that boom throwers are a wonderful, tossed salad set of characters. Playing around with the information from Ted's survey, an 11 year old boogie woogie music fan with 8 boom t-shirts could be throwing with you on one day, while a 50 year old anthropologist rock and roller owning a fish and a bird could be tossing with you on the next.

If you only take away one thing from this half serious, half humorous boomerang thrower's profile, however, it would be this: **today, the best person to start throwing boomerangs is you.**

Seventy-five collectors categorized their collections for Ted's survey: thirty-one collected anything and everything to do with booms, while twelve only collected competition boomerangs. Twelve prized artistic boomerangs, and four longed for aboriginal treasures.

Weapon: Fact or Fiction

I hope by now that I've convinced you that boomerang throwing is a sport, a sport blossoming around the country and the world. Moreover, when using common sense and proper care it is a safe sport, beautifully benign. But, how about boomerang throwing in the past? Didn't the Australians ever use it to bring home some fresh kangaroo meat?

The answer is simple. *No.*

Now, here are the slightly more detailed answers:

"Boomerangs were never intended for use as weapons, since they must be very light in order to return; too light to do any real damage to anything big enough to be a decent meal for a hungry aboriginal hunter."

...H.L. Mayhew quoting from *Boomerangs,* a 1981 publication by the Pacific Northwest Museum of Flight

"Most people are scared of the boomerang. They think it is a weapon used to kill people. That's a misconception."

...Chet Snouffer

"The main use of the returning boomerang was for amusement or sport, and not for hunting. The confusion about boomerangs being used for hunting goes all of the way back to explorer Captain Cook and his crew. The Europeans did not realize that there were different types of flying sticks with different names."

...Norm Kern

"If a bear came in your tent, which one would you rather have? A three to four pound club to swing at the bear, or a three to five ounce v-shaped piece of wood? The answer is just common sense."

...Gary Broadbent

It's a shame that one semantic mistake by Captain Cook led to all this confusion. Boomerangs aren't weapons."

...Michael Gel Girvin

"If you wanted a weapon, you'd want one you could aim. If you wanted to throw at an enemy, you'd have to throw about thirty feet to the right, and hope the boomerang would swing around and hit him. That would be pretty inefficient, and the thrower would be in big trouble when his enemy realized what he was trying to do."

...Gary Broadbent

"Good news. There are two classes of people in the world: 1) Those who know the difference between boomerang fun and heavy curved sticks for throwing and killing, and 2) Those who someday will (know the difference).

...H L Mayhew,
The Big Book About Boomerangs

Now it's *finally* time to throw.

How to Toss Like a Pro

"The history of the boomerang and the history of boomerang fun are two different histories."

"Boomeranging fun decreases in proportion to the time not spent boomeranging. This is the boomeranging law of diminishing returns."

"Here's a circular thought for today: it's more fun to run around in circles throwing and catching boomerangs than it is to run around in circles trying to search out why people run around in circles throwing and catching boomerangs."

...all said by boomerang humorist and enthusiast, H.L. Mayhew, Columbus, OH

Well, I've spent the past three years watching boomerang throwers, and writing about them for newspapers, magazines and now this book. It was definitely time for me to learn; time for me to throw the rang thing!

Standing in the midst of a grassy field on a glaringly bright spring day, gripping a thin piece of curved plastic, I was amazed at the sheer audacity of any human being who actually believed that a boomerang could return. I certainly didn't expect mine to.

Sure, I've written about these enthusiastic boom people, acting like I believed them when they told me their booms returned. When I watched them throw and catch their boomerangs, I pretended like I thought it was for real. But standing there, holding my first boomerang, I thought - no way.

Well, guess what? With a little practice, boomerangs do return -- quite accurately, in fact. And, while I have had the wonderful fortune to be taught by some of the geniuses of the boomerang world, it is possible for any determined person to learn to master the boom basics.

Location, location, location isn't only important when buying real estate; it's also vital when choosing a spot to toss the rang. The best place to throw is in a large grassy area, free of trees, telephone poles and unsuspecting spectators. Michael Gel Girvin suggests throwing in an area that is at least twice the range of the radius of the boomerang. So, if your boomerang can go out twenty meters in each direction, make sure you're in the center of an area with at least forty meters surrounding you in every direction.

When buying one of Gel's boomerangs, the range is listed on the package. He also cautions inexperienced throwers to add extra room to their playing field, until they gain control over the flight of their boomerang.

Your boomerangs shouldn't have sharp edges, and beginners should use lightweight booms. Throwing with an experienced boomeranger is a real plus, as well. Other important safety tips include throwing in adequate light, so you can always keep your eye on the boomerang, and to avoid throwing in winds over 5 miles per hour. Mayhew suggests, if you drop a tissue and it blows out of reach, then it's too windy to throw.

Chicago Bob decides the wind strength by using the *Beaufort Scale*, listing a method in his newsletter to determine wind strengths up to 38 mph. Since that is a tad too windy for our purposes, I'll just mention the relevant breezes. With the Beaufort Scale, calm is defined as "no wind, smoke rises vertically." With a light air, ranging from 1 to 3 mph, you can observe the wind direction from smoke. A light breeze (4 to 7 mph) causes the leaves to rustle and flags to flap lazily, and you can feel a light breeze on your face. Finally, a gentle breeze (8 to 12 mph) causes leaves and small twigs to constantly be in motion, and the flag is extended. If the day is windier, definitely leave it to the experts to handle.

Okay, now back to the safety tips. Children should have adult supervision with boomerangs, and if a boomerang is heading in the direction of another person, yell "Boom!" loudly and clearly, much as you would yell "Fore!" when a golf ball was sailing towards another golfer on a course.

Never try catching a boomerang that is diving towards the ground, higher than chest level, or that is returning at a rapid speed. For extra protection, you should wear eye protection and gloves.

Now the boomerang itself. First, make sure you buy a quality boomerang. While a decent wooden boomerang could cost you between $10 and $30, those "terrific deal" boomerangs almost inevitably have one tiny flaw: they don't return. This isn't to say, however, that there aren't quality non-wooden boomerangs for under $10. Eric Darnell, Gary Broadbent and Gregg Snouffer, for example, all make foam and/or plastic ones that work well, including models that can be safely thrown indoors. I started throwing with the non-wooden ones, but the important factor is to always consider your source when buying a boom.

Experienced throwers laugh about instructions that they used to find inside packages of toy boomerangs — those directions that suggest you experiment with sidearm, or overhead techniques, or ones that are so ridiculous that you could never get the boomerang to fly.

"That explains many of the comments that I hear," Chet Snouffer said. "Ones like - I had a boomerang as a kid. It didn't work."

Instead, follow these directions, ones provided by the best throwers in the world today. Stretch and warm-up first. The 1995 United States Open Division Champ Norm Kern starts by swinging his arm around several times, then he goes through a dozen or so throwing motions without a boom in his hand.

Then, for the last few mock throws, he holds two or three boomerangs, much like a baseball batter swinging two bats in the on-deck circle. "Then, I start throwing with a short range boom," Norm said, "and on the first few throws it might not come all the way back. Eventually, I get warmed up."

In MTA tournaments, where the thrower only tosses once every four minutes, he loads all his MTAs in a sock, swinging it with his throwing arm to stay loose. Before *trick catching*, *doubling*, *endurance* and *fast catch*, he goes through the throwing motion a few minutes before his turn arrives.

Once you're ready to go, make sure the curved painted side of the boom is closest to you. In flight, the curved side is the top, and the flat side is the bottom. You can grab either arm of a two bladed boomerang, the two arms being known as the dingle arm and the lift arm. With a three bladed boom, you can grab any arm, as well. If you're left handed, however, make sure you're throwing a lefty rang.

If you have a plastic or foam, easily tunable boom, this is what you can do. Twist the left side of each arm down if you're left handed, and twist down the right side if you're a righty.

Use the wind to your advantage. Right handed people want the wind on their left cheek, while a lefty wants to feel it on the right cheek. Gary Broadbent sets up an antenna tied with a floaty strip of material, so he can easily see the direction of the wind.

The two basic boomerang grips are the pinch grip and the pistol grip. To use the pinch grip, make a fist, pinching the boomerang between the index finger and thumb. Girvin suggests making a hitchhiking sign first, then pinching the rang tightly.

For the pistol grip, wrap your thumb, index finger and middle finger around the boomerang, like holding a pencil. The first finger hooks around the edge of the boomerang.

Whichever way you choose, make sure you hold your boomerang up and down, not horizontally like a frisbee. Before throwing, your boom should be almost vertical when released, never tipping to the side more than five to twenty degrees.

Okay, I'd followed those directions at home, in my backyard with a boom specially designed for small spaces. I'd thrown the boomerang and it would fly out, curving a little ways, but then it crashed. Big time. Either I had a defective boomerang, or I was an utter failure at throwing. My opinion about which it was kept changing by the minute.

Then, I headed to Canton, Ohio, to Gary Broadbent's house. For a couple of hours, I watched him throw amazing distances, making incredible catches. No matter how many times I've watched him throw, I'll never get used to seeing how a boomerang flies in the hands of a master.

But, then, Gary handed me a lightweight, three bladed boomerang, tuning it for me. No more spectator sporting for me. I

Pick up pieces of grass and test the wind's direction. You want to face about 45 degrees away from the wind.

grabbed the boomerang, and — Gary stopped me. *Wrong.*

Wrong? Me? Couldn't be. The sun had to be in Gary's eyes.

"Hold the boomerang in the shape of a Y," he said.

I already was.

"Now," he added, "make sure Mr. Y is tired."

I tipped the left side of the boomerang back, so one arm almost touched my forearm. Oops, I guess wasn't doing that. A tiny detail, but I found out details are pretty important when tossing a rang.

Next, you're supposed to pick a point on the horizon, like a tree (or in my case, the building where the disc golf award ceremony was taking place, and where Gary's enterprising children were selling cups of water for 25 cents, because the water fountain broke) and I aimed a little above the horizon. I pulled my arm back over my shoulder, with my wrist bent backwards.

Next, I extended my arm fully while throwing, and I tossed straight up and down. Experienced throwers compare it to throwing a baseball pitch, never like a sidearm, frisbee-like throw. Imitate throwing a tomahawk or cracking a whip. A strong snap of the wrist will create spin, which is even more important than power.

Right handed throwers need to throw in a counterclockwise direction. Use Bud Pell's creative poetry to remind yourself of the correct flight pattern:

```
                     COME,  WILL
             AS                   IT
         IF                         'ROUND
         IT'S                         AND
       ON                              FAR
       A                                OUT
     HIDDEN                            GOES
     STRAND                             IT
     IT                                FUN,
       COMES                         SOME
       RIGHT                         HAVE
         BACK                        TO
         TO                        BOOM
           MY                      MY
         HAND.              THROWING
                  WHEN
```

Lefties, however, throw in a clockwise direction. Then, you're off and running.

I threw mine a few times that way. It curved maybe three quarters of the way around the circular pattern, then it crashed. Gary suggested that I step forward with my right foot (remember, I'm a lefty), to give the toss more *oomph*.

And, it worked. While behind me, Gary was tossing MTAs high into the dazzling sky, then tossing quick booms, and flinging himself on the ground to do wild foot catches, my little boomerang flew out a few feet, just a few feet off the ground, and then it made a cute little circle and returned to me.

I even *caught it*.

For a brief second in time, my sweet circle appeared even more miraculous than anything else I'd seen - because I'd done it myself. Gary ran over to congratulate me, and pronounced me an official boom babe; a little prematurely, probably, but it was an incredibly exciting moment, anyhow.

My husband, Don and the photographer, Len, have moved onto experimenting with competition boomerangs, with Gary offering plenty of useful tips for them, as well. They both plan to start tossing in the open division tournaments this year and next, so they wanted more detailed competitive advice.

'BOUT BOOMS *Author Kelly Boyer Sagert lines up her first ever toss*

I'm almost positive that I didn't hear Gary telling my husband, "booms before babes," though. You didn't tell him that, Gary, did you?

I'm sure he didn't, so let's just move onto the boomerang catch. Observe the flight of your boomerangs, to watch its timing. Then, to catch the boomerang, you make a boomerang sandwich, holding one hand above and one hand below the boom, palms parallel with the approaching boom. If everything goes right, it will glide into your hands. When it does, slap your hands together.

You never know who you'll meet when you're tossing boomerangs. While I was taking lessons from Gary, people young and old approached him, asking him about his marvelous magical stick.

When one man saw Gary, he pulled two MTA rangs from his back pocket, and yelled, "Hey - don't just stand there. Throw that thing!"

Gary laughed, started to make a smart-alecky response, then threw his hands up in amazement. "Red! I don't believe it! It's Red Whittington!"

Red, a former boomerang thrower who competed in USBA tournaments from 1982 until 1987, hadn't seen Gary in nine years. Since that time, Gary and Red had both moved, and they'd lost touch with each other.

"Red practically invented the freestyle throwing that is standard with throwers today," Gary explained. "He created the *flamingo catch*, where one leg is up in the air, and you reach around the leg on the ground to catch the boomerang. Red is more flexible than Gumby."

In his peak year of boomerang throwing, Red was 9th in the nation, snagging a second place finish in the MTA. He earned a reputation as the guy who could toss a rang, flip up in the air for a two and a half twister, then catch the stick.

After his boom retirement in 1987, however, Red focused more on disc golf, earning the 1991 Professional Disc Golf Association Masters World Championship.

In an amazing coincidence, Red was competing in a disc golf tournament on a course right behind the park where we were throwing boomerangs. While competing, someone told Red that people were tossing rangs in the park.

"I figured the throwers were a bunch of novices, and so I came over to watch," Red said, with a laugh. "When I got closer, I realized that the man wearing the USA jacket was no beginner."

As he approached Gary, he suddenly recognized his friend from years ago. "What a blast from the past!" Gary said. "It's just unbelievable." So, not only did I get to watch Gary throw that day, I also got to watch the incredible Red Whittington in action.

Red Whittington Pioneer Rang-er

One thing both throwers had in common is that they learn from their mistakes. And just like Gary kept encouragingly shouting on the field that day, "make sure you learn from every single throw."

If the boomerang climbs then crashes, for example, you're not throwing up and down, and if that's the case, I sympathize with you. This is called too much layover.

If your boomerang doesn't spin in a complete circle, you probably didn't throw hard enough. Pick a point just above the horizon and rethrow, making sure your wrist snaps to impart the necessary spin. Again, by the way, I sympathize with you. Either I'm a real sympathetic kind of person, or a lousy boomerang thrower. Or both.

If the boomerang lands behind you, throw more away from the wind. If it circles, but lands in front of you, throw more directly into the wind. If the boom flies past you, ease up, or try a more vertical position.

If the boomerang fails to climb and then it hits the ground, make sure you're gripping the curved side towards you, and that you've got the correct boomerang for whatever hand you're throwing with.

Competitive throwers often weight their boomerangs to adjust for wind conditions, by taping coins on the underside of their boomerang, or by snapping on rubber bands or by clipping on a paper clip. This takes plenty of experimentation, to find out what works best for you.

Got all that? If so, there is a huge world out there for you, complete with trick catches behind your back and with your feet, speed throwing, accuracy throwing, and other competitive events. While there is more of that in the next chapter, I'd like to list some boomerang games here, ones played just for the fun of it.

Humor me here, however, and let me digress. I promise I'll return to the subject shortly. When I was about eight or nine, a neighborhood friend of mine invented a great game. He drew two boxes in the soft dirt with a stick, then he climbed into a tree. All of the neighborhood kids, along with my mother and my friend's mother, each bet on which box he'd land in. Several of us won our bet; my friend, however, broke his arm in his spiralling dive.

Looking back, I believe our game lacked common sense. We didn't learn much from that lesson, however, as later we got stuck on a garage roof while playing hide and go seek, and then, later still, I smashed my back tooth in a swinging game of croquet.

My point? Choose your games wisely, with a large dose of common sense thrown in.

That said, there's a great game called **GLORP**, with Michael Gel a commanding GLORP-er. In it, the leader, known as the *dominator*, throws a boomerang and makes a trick catch. All other players must duplicate his or her type of catch. If you miss, you get a letter of the word GLORP.

When the dominator misses his catch, the next player becomes dominator. The dominator, however, does not receive a letter for that miss. The last remaining player, a **GLOR** if the game has been exciting, is the winner.

Usually, the thrower with the least amount of experience is the first dominator, with the person with the next least amount leading next. Once all people have had the position of dominator, the first thrower becomes dominator again.

The dominator is allowed to make a regular, non-trick catch. If he does that, however, that counts as a pass onto the next dominator, with no letters assigned for the pass. In other words, that is how someone can skip a turn as dominator, and he does not receive any kind of penalty for the pass.

However, when a dominator passes, the other throwers can take over the dominatorship by successfully performing a trick catch. The first thrower to do so becomes the new dominator, with the other throwers required to duplicate the successful trick catch. In addition, the same trick catch cannot be performed on consecutive turns.

Once you have missed five catches, you've been G-L-O-R-P-ed and you're out of the game.

Besides the popular game of GLORP, other throwers celebrate their holidays with boomerangs. Chet Snouffer, for example, celebrates New Year's Eve by throwing the boom before midnight, and catching it after the new year rings in.

Norm Kern, a former USBA board member, loves boomerang games, also creating holiday entertainment. Norm led the team of throwers that created the *Super Novice* tournament rules, sort of a tournament-lite. Some examples of Super Novice are listed in the next section of this book, but here's a snapshot of Norm's innovative gaming style:

He suggests having a November *Turkey Toss* for the day after Thanksgiving, and he recommends hot chocolate for the chosen refreshment. He also likes playing the *Aussie Rag* game that day. Each person throws from the rag fastened to the ground. If you catch your boomerang, you take three steps towards the rag, starting from where you snagged the rang. If you miss, you stay where your boomerang landed.

Whoever ends up closest to the rag wins the round, and throws first in the next round. "This event has enough competition to keep things interesting, but not enough to cause much ill will," Norm said.

He also enjoys a June *Summer Soltice* throw. On the longest day of the year, Norm and friends throw until about 11 p.m., adding light sticks once the darkness falls. The light sticks are plastic, transparent and a little flexible. When you bend them, there is a chemical reaction inside and it emits light. While there are boomerangs specially created with slots for the sticks, most people attach them to the inside of the trailing arm of the boom with transparent tape. Norm said the taping doesn't affect most medium or large boomerangs, although you will have to throw them harder to overcome the additional drag.

Later that soltice night, everyone signs a boomerang, and the autographed stick is awarded to someone who has recently made a terrific contribution to the boom world. If you and your friends sign a boomerang, you could think of your own way to award the rang.

You could gift it to the person who creates the best new game for the next boom bash, or to whoever writes the best boom poem. Or, for an even more equal opportunity contest, hand it to the person who writes the worst boomerang poem. In that case, though, it might be tough to choose the winner.

Norm enjoys hearing about games that others create, although he'll probably cringe when he reads my "who keeps the boom" suggestions. If you have ideas for boomerang games, please pass them along to me and I'll make sure Norm gets them.

Who knows? The person who starts the next great boomerang game craze just might be you.

Tournament Events

Something you should know right away: One meter equals 39.37 inches, only slightly longer than one yard. Fifty (50) yards, half a football field is about 46 meters.

Okay, now that you've absolutely perfected those throwing skills, you're ready to move into the tournament world, right?

Or, if you're like Chicago Bob, you could always place second in a tournament and win an individual event first, then you could practice throwing a boomerang. But, either way, here are the basics of the seven standard tournament events.

ACCURACY:

I THREW MY BOOMERANG
INTO THE AIR,
AND WHEN IT LANDS I
KNOW NOT WHERE.
THAT'S NOT TOO SWIFT, AS
YOU SHALL SEE,
'CAUSE I'M THROWING IN
ACCURACY.

The simplest is **Accuracy**. The USBA compares it to playing darts, but you throw from inside of the bullseye. You throw five times from the bullseye, out twenty meters, then let the boom land, hopefully in the center of your target. A perfect landing receives 10 points, so a perfect score is 50. The person with the most points wins this event.

Gregg Snouffer pointed out that, although there have been several scores of 48, and a couple of 49, the perfect 50 has still eluded even the best of the throwers.

AUSSIE ROUND:

AUSSIE'S MY FAVORITE,
I THROW VERY LONG,
THE HOOK CIRCLES 'ROUND
HUMMING ITS SONG.
IT SAILS OVER HEAD, I'M
FOLLOWING FINE,
AND MAKE A
DIVING CATCH OVER
THE FIFTY METER LINE.

The Australian Round, also known as the **Aussie Round**, gets a bit more complicated. It adds distance and catching ability to the mix. A throw tossed out 50 meters gets the maximum distance points of 6; a 20 meter toss is the shortest legal throw. A bullseye still scores 10 points, and a catch nets you another 4 points. Again, the most points wins, with an absolutely perfect Aussie Round, your score would be 100.

While this has never been achieved in any competition, the Moleman boasts an astonishing current World Record score of 95.

Okay, let's pick up the speed. **Fast Catch** involves making 5 throws and 5 catches as quickly as possible with the same boomerang. The world record of 14.60 seconds is one of the most amazing feats in the boomerang world today. Try the fast catch sometime to get a feel for how lightening fast that record really is.

In **Endurance** you test your fast catching ability over a period of five minutes, tossing and catching the same boomerang as many times as possible, starting from the bullseye.

Maximum Time Aloft, or the MTA event, has the opposite feel to it. After throwing a boomerang high into the air, you hope it whizzes around up there for as long as possible before you make your catch. If you don't catch the descending rang, the throw doesn't count.

While the official world record is just under three minutes, John Gorski tossed a boomerang after an official tournament ended, and he was clocked at an awesome 17 minutes, 6 seconds. His isn't the only incredible MTA tale, however. Larry Ruhf's 1986 throw will also live on in boomerang folklore.

Ruhf tossed his boomerang, watching it disappear over a group of trees. Following the rang, he watched it head over a highway. As Ruhf crossed the busy road, the rang flew over a railroad trestle. Racing underneath the trestle, he watched the boomerang descend into a peaceful, unsuspecting neighborhood, a fifth of a mile from his original spot.

Standing out in the middle of the road, he snagged the boomerang, breaking the world record at that time, with his MTA toss of 2 minutes and 31 seconds.

Trick Catch adds spice and color to the tournament. You'll see catches from behind the back, under the leg and with the feet, with twelve trick catches in each event. I plan to avoid practicing any of these while the neighbors are watching.

Every competitor who makes twelve successful trick catches moves on to the throw-offs. All qualifiers toss the throw-offs at the same time, rotating the four designated trick catches until a boomerang is missed. The person making the most consecutive catches wins the event.

Last of all is **Doubling**, where you toss two boomerangs at one time. One flies fairly levelly, while the other rises. "They shouldn't just be separated," cautions Gary Broadbent. "They should be divorced."

The booms return about the same time, and you catch them in rapid succession. If you can't hold onto the first boomerang until after the second is caught, the first catch doesn't count. There are six rounds in this event; the fourth round, for example, includes one of the doubled boomerangs caught behind the back and the other under the leg.

Juggling used to be an official event, where the thrower alternates boomerangs, in a juggling style. Chet Snouffer tossed an incredible 502 boomerangs, a world record just recently broken by Yannick Charles of France, who threw 555 juggling tosses.

FAST CATCH:

I LET IT GO WITH
ALL MY MIGHT,
ITS BLAZING SPEED WAS
QUITE A SIGHT.
I LINED IT UP AND
REACHED OUT FAST,
BY THEN MY FAST CATCH
WAS FIVE FEET PAST.

ENDURANCE:

I TAKE A DEEP BREATH FOR
THROWING THIS ROUND.
I JUMP AND I LEAP AND DIVE
TO THE GROUND.
I THROW AND I THROW FOR
A VERY LONG TIME,
"WHAT DO YOU MEAN I
ONLY CAUGHT NINE!!"

MTA:

I CHUCKED MY MTA
UP IN THE SKY;
IT SPIRALLED UP AND
CAME OUT HIGH.
IT CAME IN SPINNING WITH
HARDLY A SOUND,
AND STUCK THE DINGLE
ARM DEEP IN THE GROUND.

TRICK CATCH:

I FLICKED MY WRIST,
THE BOOM WENT 'ROUND.
COMING BACK GOOD BUT
FELL TO THE GROUND.
IT BOUNCED OFF
MY KNUCKLES, MY ELBOW
AND THIGH,
NOR COULD I CATCH
WITH MY FEET, I DON'T
KNOW WHY.

DOUBLING:

TWO AT ONCE IS
QUITE A CHORE,
'CAUSE THE OLD ARM ENDS
UP SO SORE.
I WATCH THEM GO 'ROUND
AND RUN TO THE SPOT,
AND DROP LEFT AND RIGHT,
AS IF THEY WERE HOT.

JUGGLING:

THE FINAL EVENT IS
JUGGLING, YOU KNOW.
FIRST ONE THEN THE OTHER,
YOU CATCH AND
YOU THROW.
THE START IS SO EASY,
THEN THREES AND FOURS-
"HOW COULD I POSSIBLY
END UP WITH YOURS?"

Got it? The USBA puts out an official handbook, with precise event rules and scoring. USBA rules are followed in tournament events, with tournament officials making any difficult calls. The book defines legal catches and the size of the bullseye in certain events, for example, along with each contestant's rights and obligations. The price for this rulebook is $2, and the USBA address is listed in the resource chapter of this book. For a tournament to be recognized by the USBA, the events must be run in compliance with all their rules. Eleven or more veteran throwers must participate, the field requirements must be met and the events must run in the order that they were advertised, announced and submitted.

People may also enter a tournament in the open category, due to inexperience, age or other criteria that are set out in the tournament flyer. A person cannot compete in the same tournament as both an open and a veteran.

In a recent USBA newsletter, officers provided their **Super Novice** Rules, scaled down to "provide a positive recreational and learning setting for beginning throwers - AKA to make sure everyone has fun!" Rating scales are the same as for the veteran events. The Super Novice winner receives 11 points, with the second place contestant receiving 9, and every person receiving one less point all the way down. In the event of a tie, the points are equally split between the tied individuals.

Super Novice events are less demanding, however. While the thrower must make a good attempt to "create gyroscopic precession," there are no minimum distances required in any of the events. In the trick catch, for example, the thrower must toss eight rangs. Each touched but not caught boom earns one point, a catch earns two points and a one-handed catch or trap garners three points. A one-handed backhand equals four points, a behind the back or under the leg equal five points, and a one-handed behind the back or under the leg earns seven points.

The granddaddy of all catches, the foot catch gathers ten points. Then, participants total their scores for the event, ranking themselves in order. Then, the actual event points are disregarded, and the winner receives 11 points for the first place finish, the second place contestant receives 9 points, and so on.

There are six modified Super Novice tournament events in all. After totalling the assigned place points after all scheduled events, the rankings should be apparent.

Here are some of the other event variations. In a "limited" version of a fast throw, the participant throws five times, with the stop watch starting upon the first throw. There is no minimum distance requirement for the boomerang to travel, however, in order for the throw to count.

The stop watch clicks off after the fifth boomerang and the thrower are back at the starting point. Catches are optional, and there is only one round. The shortest time wins.

In a "fast throw endurance," each participant throws for two minutes; again, catching is not required, although the thrower must make an attempt for circular flight. The timer should warn the thrower at specific time intervals: when there is "one minute remaining," "thirty seconds remaining" and "fifteen seconds remaining." Then, the timer should count down the last ten seconds. Whoever throws the most earns the first place points for that event.

For the "maximum time aloft limited," the thrower can use any boomerang except for a MTA boom. Each thrower tosses three consecutive times, and a stop watch times from the moment of release until the thrower either touches the boomerang, or the rang lands. The thrower uses his or her longest time of the three throws, if the boomerang was not touched. If the boomerang was touched, but not caught by the thrower, two seconds are added on to the time of the longest throw. If the thrower catches the boomerang, then four seconds are added to the longest throw.

See you in Sydney, 2000!

Talk the Talk - Boom Glossary

Okay, so you can walk the boomerang walk, toss the boomerang toss — now, it's time to learn to talk the boomerang talk.

Boomerang throwers, like any other group, salt, pepper and otherwise spice up their language with slang. Some slang is taken from more widespread usage, while other words are uniquely used in the boomerang world.

The positive attitude of boom tossers shines through, even in their vocabulary. While Mother Nature regularly plays practical jokes on these dedicated throwers, the great majority of their slang refers to the incredibly awesome events of the day.

While the slang vocabulary is constantly growing, there are some words that you'll almost always hear at a boom tourney. Boomerangs, for example, are often called something other than boomerangs. You'll hear talk of a "B," or a "*boom*" or a "*rang.*"

Then, there are specific types of boomerangs. Here are just two examples:

Tri-fly® - a boomerang having three wings, invented by Eric Darnell

Two-blader - the basic kind of boomerang, having two arms

Or, instead, the thrower might refer to the maker of his boomerang, as in, "Oh, are you throwing your *Chet* today? Did you bring your *Jonas*?"

And here are some of the ways you can adjust the flight of your boomerang:

Clip - a large paper clip attached to boomerang, to slow the descent of the boomerang in huge winds. Clip provides drag.

Flapage - tape such as duct or electrical that is folded over and taped onto the wings of the boomerang to slow the boomerang down, or to cause the boomerang to descend more predictably.

Swiss cheese - holes drilled in the boomerang to provide drag for windy conditions or stable descent.

There are also nicknames for specialized boom events:

Aussie Round - Australian Round - a competition event combining distance, throwing and accuracy skills.

MTA - Maximum Time Aloft - a competition event where the object is to keep the boomerang in the air as long as possible. MTA also refers to the specialized boomerang used in this event.

And, boomers often describe the quality of their throws:

Blow-by - a boomerang flying past you a great distance.

Dingle arm - a throw made by holding onto the dingle arm - if you look at the curved side of the boomerang, elbow up - the dingle arm is on the left. (only with two blader, right hand boom. Reverse for lefty boom.)

Floater - a boomerang that descends slowly, or a boomerang that has caught an updraft.

Humpback - a throw with a high release point which helps boomerang return accurately in windy conditions.

Raddest - beyond excellent. The ultimate throw or catch.

Rippa - a very good throw or catch.

Shredding - an aggressive, excellent performance.

Vertical - the opposite of horizontal, and the throwing plane in which a boomerang is released. Boomerangs are thrown vertically, while frisbees are thrown horizontally.

So, get out there and practice your throwing skills, and brush up on all this slang. Before long, you too will be an official *boom stud* or *boom babe*, aka a boomeranger with throwing prowess. Attend a *boom bash*, or have one of your own. (A boom bash is a party at which boomerang games predominate, or a gathering of boomerangers in an open field or similar good venue.)

And, soon, you'll be *stoked*! (that's a feeling, by the way, of contentment and confidence which results from being in the zone.)

I'd end this glossary with "*Stay Rad*!", but that might give away the identity of the person who helped me with this chapter!

American (A) Records
and World (W) Records

Provided by the France Boomerang Association Official Times as of October 1996.

Fast Catch:	(A) - Adam Ruhf - 14.60 seconds - 1996
	(W) - Adam Ruhf - 14.60 seconds - 1996
Maximum Catches:	(A) - Michael Gel Girvin -817-1994
	(W) - Yannick Charles of France - 1251 - 1995
Juggling:	(A) - Chet Snouffer - 502 - 1992
	(W) - Yannick Charles of France - 555 - 1995
Distance:	(A) - Jim Youngblood - 134.20 meters - 1989
	(W) - Michel Dufayard of France - 149.12 meters - 1992
Aussie Round:	(A) - John Anthony - 95 points-1995
	(W) - John Anthony - 95 points -1995
Endurance:	(A) - Adam Ruhf - 76 - 1996
	(W) - Yannick Charles of France - 76 - 1995
MTA: Unlimited:	(A) - Dennis Joyce - 2 minutes, 59 seconds - 1987
	(W) - Dennis Joyce - 2 minutes, 59 seconds - 1987
Limited:	(A) - John Anthony - 1 minute, 19 seconds - 1995
	(W) - Fridolin Frost - 1 minute, 24 seconds - 1989
Accuracy:	(A) - Mike Forrester - 49 points - 1996
	Paul David - 48 - 1991
	Dennis Joyce - 48 - 1992
	Chet Snouffer - 48 - 1993
	Will Gix - 48 - 1995
	John Flynn - 48 - 1995
	(W) - A four way tie with 49 points
	Phillipe Picgirard of France - 1990
	Joe Niederstraber of Germany - 1993
	Jurg Schedler of Switzerland - 1993
	Mike Forrester of USA - 1996

Making Your Own Boomerang

"In all the years that I've been throwing," Michael Gel Girvin said, "the greatest joy I've experienced with boomerangs happened the first day I threw out a boomerang that I had crafted, and it came back."

He had spent an hour and a half cutting and sanding his boom creation. Running out of his workshop, he threw the boom.

"It went out, then curved," Michael said, "and it came back. It came back to me."

"It was an amazing feeling that I still remember vividly. I see the same thrill in other people's faces when I teach them how to make and throw boomerangs."

And, here we are. It's time to make your own boomerang. Materials used have ranged from wood to paper and cardboard, from bone to metal, from fiberglass to foam and plastics.

Here is a set of directions that doesn't require a saw. These were given to me by Chet Snouffer.

You'll need two paint paddles used to stir newly opened cans of paint, a hot melt glue gun and a wood file. First, take the wood file and one paddle. When you look down at the wood, consider that the top side. Sand the left and right sides of the top, down the entire length of the paddle. The slope you create should be between 30 and 45 degrees.

The bottom side will remain flat and straight. Repeat the procedure with the other paddle.

After sanding them smoothly, overlap the paddles in the middle to form an x shape. Once you make sure that both "top" sides are facing up, use the hot glue to connect the two sticks. Allow the glue to dry thoroughly, preferably overnight.

Before throwing, twist the boomerang. If you're right-handed, hold the boom firmly in the center of the x, with one arm pointed towards you. Gently twist the wingtip so the right side is bent up. Do this with all four wings.

For a lefty boom, gently bend the left side up on the wings. Cross sticks don't work well in too much wind, so test this boom in calmer conditions for best results.

Test fly the boomerang, then paint and decorate your successful creation. Be sure to sign and date the boomerang, as well, so you can compare future efforts to the first one. While the successive boomerangs will most likely fly better than the first, none brings quite as much excitement as your earliest returner.

Safety Caution:

Before you throw your newly crafted boom, reread the chapter on How to Throw, and heed the safety recommendations. Invest in a pair of protective goggles and have fun, but remember common sense and safety first.

The Physics of Boomerangs

"My friends' boomerangs always fly better than mine unless I throw them." ...Beat Aepli and Bruno Bucher in their Murphy's Rules for Boomerangers

"Much has been written about what makes a boomerang go out and return. Current knowledge explains maybe 80 percent of the phenomenon. The other 20 percent is anyone's speculation."
...John Mauro, Captain,
1984 US Boomerang Team

Now that you've made your own boomerang, aren't you curious about how it works? H.L. Mayhew poetically describes a two-blader as a pair of airplane wings turning cartwheels.

Okay, the scientific version is slightly more complicated, I admit, but as long as you understand Bernoulli's Principle of Lift, gyroscopic precession, centripetal force and a few other detailed laws of physics, you should at least understand the basics of how a boomerang flies.

Hey - don't you dare put this book down! Come on, just say it three times, really fast - Bernoulli's Principle of Lift, gyroscopic precession, centripetal force, Bernoulli's Principle of Lift, gyroscopic precession, centripetal force, Bernoulli's Principle of Lift, gyroscopic precession, centripetal force. . .

Still not convinced you can understand how a boomerang works? Well, if you've seen an airplane fly, you've seen Bernoulli's Principle of Lift in action; if you can ride a bike, you can figure out gyroscopic precession, and if you can make a basketball spin on one finger, you're well on your way to understanding centripetal force.

Here goes.

If you've got a two-bladed boomerang, why don't you get it out now - it'll make the explanation a little easier to understand. If not, that's okay, too.

With the traditional boomerang, you'll see a lead wing and a trailing wing, joined in somewhat of a V shape. Each of the two wings have a leading edge and a trailing edge, the blunter leading edge always hitting the air first. A typical boomerang would have an angle of about 105 degrees between the wings.

When thrown, a typical boomerang gradually rises as it makes its circle, and then hovers for a gentle landing on the return. While the boomerang starts in a nearly vertical position, it gradually lays over until it is parallel to the ground upon the completion of its circle.

Okay, so your boomerang cuts through the air, spinning arm over arm, like a carousel with two horses might behave if tipped on the side.

If you pick up another object and throw it (not that I recommend you do that, you understand), gravity will pull that object down to the ground sooner rather than later.

A force called lift, however, keeps boomerangs from similarly crashing to the ground. And, what causes this amazing force? An airfoil, which is any shape which produces lift as it flies through the air.

Now, look at your boomerang. You'll notice that the top surface of the boomerang is curved, and the bottom of the boomerang is flat. They have the same basic shape as airplane wings.

Airfoil

As the boomerang cuts through the air, the air molecules are separated at the leading edge of the airfoil. While the air on the bottom of the boomerang has a shorter distance to travel, the air molecules on the top must move faster. Bernoulli's Principle of Lift says that an increase in speed causes a decrease in pressure, in order to keep the intrinsic energy of the air constant.

In other words, there is less air pressure on the top of the boomerang than on the bottom, because of the difference in speed, so the boomerang experiences a net lift force in an up direction out of the curved upper surface.

With me so far? It's okay if this is a little rough going. It took me at least — well, I won't say how many times I had to ask questions about this subject, but I will reveal that the number is somewhere between one and one million. And, I'm quite sure Ted Bailey's and Gary Broadbent's lips are sealed on the subject, as well.

Okay, we've touched on Bernoulli's Principle of Lift. Now, let's talk about gyroscopic precession. What is a gyroscope?

A gyroscope is a disk or wheel that spins about an axis relative to a stationary reference plane, and is free to turn in multiple directions. If you spin the gyroscope about it's axis, you can set it down on a flat surface and watch it stay upright. Even if you try to tip it, the gyroscope resists. It doesn't want to tilt.

While you're riding your bike, then, you can keep your bike in an upright position. If the wheels are not moving, however, and you try to keep your bike upright, you will get hurt. It is about as silly a game as my friend's spiralling-out-of-a-tree game, with the same probable results.

According to my experts, gyroscopic stability is the tendency of a spinning object to continue spinning about a fixed axis. The boomerang, however, experiences something called gyroscopic precession. (You're probably thinking - I know, I know - don't you remember that you made us repeat that phrase three times!)

Anyhow, let's go back to the spinning gyroscope. If you press quite hard on the spinning device, the gyroscope will tilt, but not in the manner common sense would say it should.

If you press on the right side, for example, the gyroscope would tilt forward. If you push on the back, it will tilt to the right, always in a ninety degree angle in the direction of spin.

This is gyroscopic precession.

Okay, so when you toss your boomerang, it spins almost vertically, with gyroscopic stability keeping it vertical, like a bicycle wheel. The lower pressure on the upper surface of the boomerang creates a lifting force that is directed to the left on a right-handed boomerang. A slight tilt adds enough lift in the vertical direction, straight up, to counteract gravity.

According to David Robson in his book **Why Boomerangs Return**, a typical boomerang is moving forward about 30 mph, with the arms developing a spinning speed of about 40 mph. The relative wind speed at the top of the boomerang is about 70 mph, the bottom only 10 mph.

Therefore, the lift is not evenly distributed throughout the boomerang surface. The wind speed has increased at the top, and decreased at the bottom, so there is a push from the top of the boomerang, causing it to want to flip upside down.

However, with gyroscopic precession, the push on the top is felt 90 degrees in the direction of the spin, causing the right handed boomerang to turn to the left.

Do you finally feel like we're getting somewhere? We've got the boomerang lifted in the air, we've got it spinning and now we're turning.

The boomerang is now getting ready to flatten. The almost vertical spinning stick will lay down horizontally. The boomerang, like any spinning object, rotates around its center of gravity. In a two bladed boomerang, that center is near the base of the V.

There is plenty of discussion over why a boomerang flattens the way it does. I've heard two main schools of thought; one is that the principle of lift will also naturally cause the boomerang to layover as it loses it's force.

Robson offers another thought. Here's a summary: Now, the first arm, or the leading arm, of the boomerang creates turbulence, a disturbance in the air. The second arm, the trailing or dingle arm, has to cut through the turbulence left behind, so the first arm always flies through the air at a quicker rate. If a complete rotation of the boomerang took a theoretical four seconds, for example, the time to rotate from the first leading wing to the second trailing wing would take only one of those seconds, and the time from the second trailing arm back to the first leading arm would take up the next three seconds.

The leading arm, flying through nice clean air, produces more lift than the turbulent air the second arm must contend with. This is comparable to allowing one child to play in a clean room, then

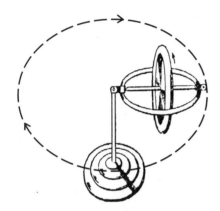

Gyroscopic Precession

letting a second child play in the not so clean room. The first child can run through the room much more efficiently than the second one. Trust me on the kid thing; I speak from experience.

The more I learn about how a basic two bladed boomerang flies, the more in awe I am of the sheer genius of people like Ted Bailey, Eric Darnell, and all the other boomerang innovators. Just amazing.

Now, here, I want to stop to take a vote. How many readers now want to move on to further, more complicated, more intricate, more controversial theories on how the boomerang works? Those of you please raise your hand. Hmm - I said please raise your hand. . .

Okay, now who wants to end this chapter with a verse or two about the magic of boomerangs? Hands down the winner. I'm surprised.

So, let me leave you with other more poetic, albeit less scientific thoughts:

GLIDING SWIFTLY THROUGH THE AIR
DESTINED FOR WHENCE IT BEGAN
THE ARCH, NO LESS THAN PERFECT
PERFORMED ONLY AS THE BOOMERANG CAN.

...Joe Conley, poet

I YIELD
AS I LAUNCH MY BOOMERANG INTO THE AIR,
I THINK OF THE MANY WHO REALLY DO CARE
IF THE BOOM LAYS OVER, OR WHY IT GOES HIGH
WHY IT TRAVELS A CIRCLE, WHY, WHY, WHY

MY TIME FOR RESEARCH IS VIRTUALLY NIL
AND I DON'T BUILD MY BOOMS WITH A GREAT DEAL OF SKILL
SO FOR ME, IT'S NECESSARY TO BOW AND YIELD
TO THE SKILLS OF BAILEY, SNOUFFER AND MAYFIELD.

...Bud Pell, poet

Boom Collectibles
(From Ted Bailey's Archives)

Boom Collage
(From Michael "Gel" Girvin's Collection)

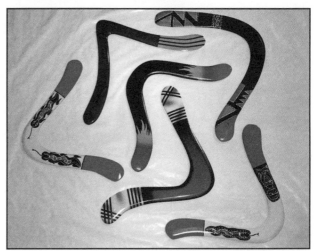

Boom Assemblage (From Ted Bailey's Collection)

Booms by the Janetzki Brothers (Les & Arthur) Australian booms showing Skippys, Admiral's Hat, Hooks, Pintubi, and Red Baron designs (Ted Bailey Collection)

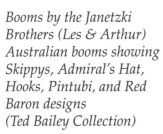

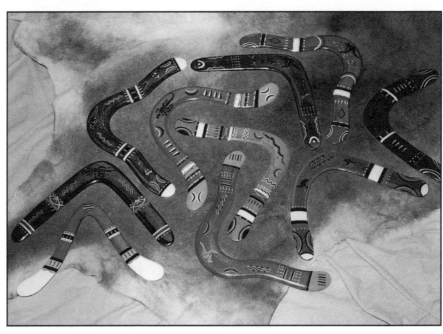

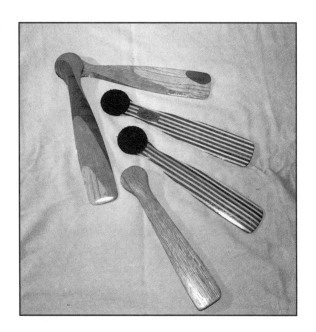

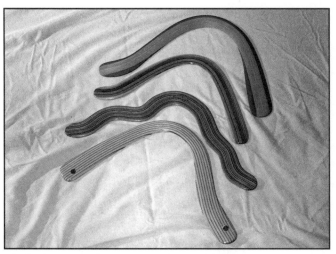

Strip-laminated Booms made in Germany

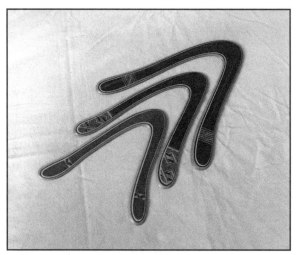

France's Didier Bonin Booms

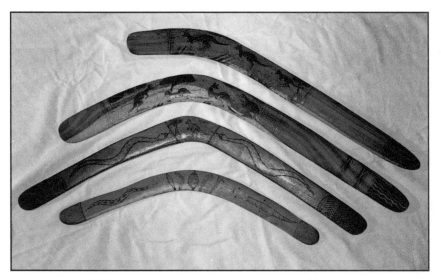

*Design Variations by
Australian Jackie Bians*

The Art of the Boomerang

"There is no question that boomerangs have art-like properties. Not only can one make boomerangs of beautiful and diverse shapes and colors and from any of multitudinous materials to create a stationary work of art, but all boomerangs when thrown create their own visual and temporal art form as they carve an ephemeral 3D sculpture in the medium of the air and nature. They will always be a unique expression of the human spirit."
...Tony Brazelton, boomerang thrower

Fred Malmberg

Blistered mahogany, with golden streaks intermingled with swirling cocoa brown...

Pink ivory, the wood from an African tree so rare that they belonged to chieftains in ages past, its appearance like a fine cherry wood aged one hundred years...

Black Rose, the Rose of the Mountain forever imprinted in the heart of the wood...

These are only some of the precious woods Dr. Fredric Malmberg chooses to create his cherished boomerangs. Then, he uses extraordinary care in their crafting. "Although most hardware stores only sell sandpaper with grit particles as fine as 600, I polish my boomerangs with sandpaper of 12,000," Fred said. "Once, when I was polishing my boomerang inlaid with mother of pearl, I noticed a black dot that I couldn't get rid of. Finally, I realized it was the wattage number on my light bulb reflecting off the shine of my boomerang."

With a quality crafted boomerang, you should be able to run a finger along the edges of the boomerang and feel no rough spots at all. "Tactile sensation is an overlooked aspect of boomerang art," he said. "Boomerangs should feel good, too."

Fred was the 1993 co-champion in the boomerang construction category, the only year the international competition was held. He tied with Sweden's Jonas Romblad.

In every year that the aesthetics contest has been held by the United States Boomerang Association, Fred's boomerangs have placed first or second, with one of his creations selling for the highest amount of money ever at a recent USBA boomerang auction.

Fred is particular about his wood. "Any time I make a boomerang out of blistered mahogany, it is automatically sold," he said. "Only the first six inches of bark blisters, so the wood is hard to come by. I also use African mahogany, quilted mahogany and curly mahogany."

Another favorite is pink ivory, wood from a tree unrelated to any other tree on earth. "Each tree sends out something in the soil that prevents any other pink ivory from growing within a twenty mile radius," Fred explained.

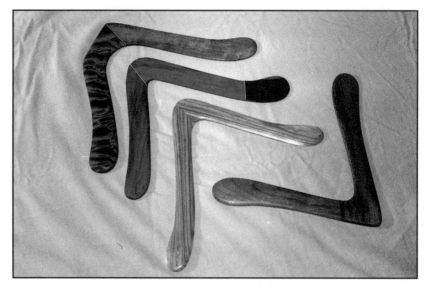

Malmberg Booms
-highly cherished by throwers and collectors

The most unusual wood, in his opinion though, is the Black Rose. "This tree grows in an oval shape, rather than a round one," he continued. "And, in each tree, around the fourth or fifth growth circle, is a rose."

"When first cut, the wood takes on multiple shades of rose, mixed in with light cocoa browns," he said. "As it oxidizes, you lose some of the rainbow; the lighter colors darken. One of the joys of woodmaking is when I get the chance to see the wood in all its glory."

Jonas Romblad

And, here is the other 1993 co-champion in the boomerang construction category, Sweden's Jonas Romblad. His MTA boomerangs are so amazing that, if you order one, you'll receive it in about 18 months. Yes, *eighteen months*. That is how long the waiting list is, for just one single boomerang.

Jonas is highly in demand for his knowledge of aerodynamics. After receiving a degree in electronics from Fredrikabremer Skolan in 1990, he graduated in December, 1995 with a Master of Science degree in Aeronautics from the School of Vehicle Engineering at the Royal Institute of Technology. He currently works for the Aeronautical Research Institute of Sweden, the Swedish equivalent of NASA, but more geared towards aeronautics, rather than space.

"His boomerangs are the ultimate,"Gary Broadbent praised. "Jonas is a perfectionist, and he finished at the top of his class in school. He is an incredible craftsman, a vital part of the boomerang world, an absolute master."

John Gorski used a Jonas boom when he tossed his amazing 17 minute, six second MTA, and John estimates that about fifty percent of the top throwers now own at least one Jonas. "I really like his boomerangs," John admitted. "They're very forgiving."

Jonas first learned about boomerangs in 1982, at the age of 13. "I would often survey the technical and hobby related sections

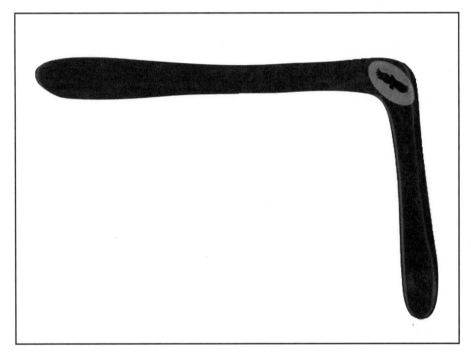

A Jonas Romblad MTA boom. His craftmanship is art!

of the local libraries," Jonas said. "I stumbled onto a book on boomerangs and I was a bit skeptical."

He and his father had recently built a small wooden dingy, and they used the leftover plywood to make a boomerang. "It worked," Jonas said, "and I had a lot of fun with it, until it got too worn to throw." He then tried to copy the boomerang, but the copy didn't work." I made a mistake with the undercut," he said, "so both booms ended up in a drawer. In 1987, I found them again and got curious; why did one work and not the other? Then, my love for experimenting took over, and I was hooked."

Jonas believes that the appeal of his MTA boomerangs is that they stay in tune. "One of the main problems with regular MTAs is that they behave like an instrument," he said, "and they have to be constantly tuned to perform as expected. With my MTAs, you don't have to do that. Also, they seem to be rather stable, and they have good performance."

He plans to continue to study the aerodynamics of boomerangs, and then to develop his MTA technology even further. He calls experimenting with boomerangs the greatest appeal about the returning stick. "One can go into the workshop and emerge an hour or two later with a world class boom, or one that won't even return," he said. "There is still no ultimate boomerang, nor a way to theoretically derive a boom with a desired flight path. There is an amazing complexity of physics around such a simple device."

Luckily, Jonas doesn't mind revealing a few boom construction tricks of the trade. "The idea is to use strong materials where strength is needed and light materials where a low weight is important," he said. "The problem is that the strong materials come in fibers, just like fabric, while the light material comes as a powder. Consequently, you need something to keep the light and strong materials together, and in just the right places."

Jonas uses a special epoxy resin for that purpose. "The black fibers you see when looking at my MTAs are carbon fibers," he said. "There is one layer with the fibers running along the boomerang arms, roughly 0.3 mm thick. Under this is a yellow or brownish layer of a weave of aramide fibers running 45 degrees to the arms, about 0.4 mm thick."

These two types of fibers, along with the epoxy matrix material form the top and bottom shell of the boom. "The cavity between the shells is filled by microballoons," he explained. "To the naked eye, this looks like a brown powder with one tenth the density of water. Under a microscope, it looks like tiny soap bubbles made from plastic. This powder is mixed with epoxy and serves as the core of the boomerang."

Jonas estimates he has made over 200 of these composite MTAs in the past five years, with approximately 100 of those ending up in the states. A full dozen of those United-States-bound boomerangs have ended up in the hands of Gary Broadbent. But, Gary has already lost eight of those to the fickle forces of the sky. Gary laments the loss of those boomerangs, and he sums up why owning a boomerang made by the Swedish genius is so important. "Without a Jonas," he said, "you will lose."

John Cryderman

John Cryderman's boomerangs are fit for a king. Or at least for a king to be.

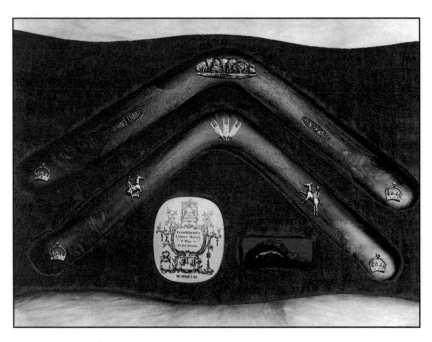

*John Cryderman's
Prince Charles Booms*

When John originally contacted the British Embassy with an idea for a royal boomerang, he received a lukewarm response. After submitting a sketch of his proposal, however, he received a phone call from the British High Commission, requesting two handcrafted boomerangs for Prince Charles.

"They're the most expensive boomerangs in the world," John said. While the actual cost of the two boomerangs was only $9,000, his 400 hours of labor would put the selling price of the donated boomerangs to $22,000.

Crafted from horizontally lapped laminated exotic woods, he carved out Prince Charles riding his polo pony. The polo stick and horse hooves were outlined with solid gold, with silver outlining the reins. Prince Charles himself sparkles with 18 karat gold. The Canadian symbol of sheaves of wheat glow with gold, as well, and the Royal Crowns at the boomerang tips were decorated with cow bone, mother of pearl and gold.

The precious boomerangs rest in a two inch thick burled walnut case, the case itself decorated with Indonesian rosewood, bronze and silver. Prince Charles himself wrote John to thank him, adding that he doubted he'd ever throw the artistic boomerangs.

John personally chooses the trees that he uses to create his boomerang art, and then he specifies how he wants the trees cut. "After the trees are sliced into boards, I store them in a type of greenhouse, because if the wood has less then twenty percent moisture, then it's difficult to work with. When I'm ready to make the boomerangs, I cut the wood into 8 or 10 inch strips. Then, I put them into steamers until they're pliable."

His customers select which of the 150 boomerang shapes they'd like their finished product to be, with 55 of these shapes totally original creations by John. He then clamps the strips into a mold, creating a two inch thick boomerang. "Of course, no boomerang this thick would fly, so I slice this into five or six quarter-inch thick boomerangs."

While a typical boomerang takes John between one week and three months to complete, he has spent up to three hundred hours on a single long distance boomerang. "When I'm finished, the boomerang is perfectly tuned, perfectly balanced, with exact air foils," he added. "It is hand honed, with even the resins and hardeners weighed first, for a perfect balance."

While he handcrafts boomerangs with high quality oak, ash, walnut and cherry, he expects you to throw and catch them. "My motto is — if you can eat a bowl of jello with a spoon — you can throw any one of my boomerangs and look like a professional thrower," John's instructions read. "They are eloquent, made like a piece of furniture, nice to have and are great for recreation and sport, and are affordable to everyone."

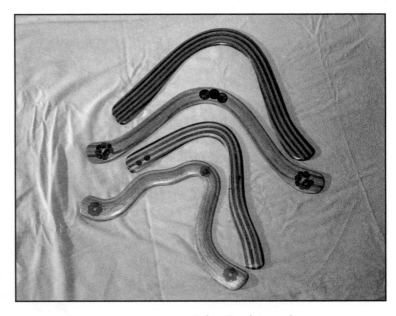

John Cryderman's strip laminated booms

A resident of Canada, Cryderman first started creating boomerangs while working as a furniture maker. "I want my boomerangs to be the Cadillac of strip laminated work," he said. "It's my specialty."

He also enjoys putting on boomerang demonstrations and workshops. "I like to explain the historical significance and the evolutionary history of the boomerang, explaining the perspective behind boomerangs versus hunting sticks," he said. "I don't want to sell a million boomerangs a year, but I'd like to help people appreciate them."

While John lives in Canada, he points to several Americans as his boomerang inspiration. "Ted Bailey is an incredibly knowledgeable man, Eric Darnell is amazing and Chet is a fantastic competitor," he said. "These guys are the cream of the crop."

Kim Deutschman

For years, Kim Deutschman, formerly of Natal, South Africa, has painted his boomerangs with Zulu and Ndebele art, with his creations called "among the most coveted art boomerangs in any collection," in the Spring 1989 issue of **Many Happy Returns**.

While he has since moved to the United States, he continues to design boomerangs rich in African culture. Colors have a special meaning for the Zulu and Ndebele tribes, and Kim uses those to "reflect traditional tribal decorations and meanings."

Red, for example, denotes intense passion, yellow symbolizes riches and wealth and white stands for purity and faithfulness. Green is for coolness and rain, and blue "can mean the thoughts that fly to the loved ones like the wings of a dove."

One of Kim's boomerangs won the best decorated category in the Atlanta Nationals in 1986. He recently started to create unusual boomerang art, by framing his highly decorated boomerangs, and hanging them on walls. He has also started painting a series of limited paintings of boomerangs on canvas.

Kim Deutschman Booms

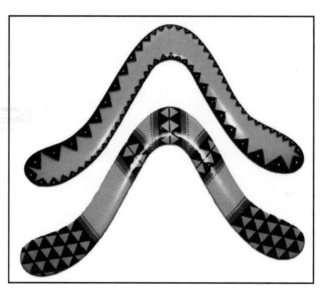

Neil Kalmanson

"The traditions of boomerang art meet in this exhibition, one as old as mankind and one newly born. Each gives us an insight into the artist's world, his sense of beauty, of place, and of spirit." ...Neil Kalmanson, boomerang thrower, poet and artist

Neil Kalmanson, an Associate Professor of Art at East Georgia College and the director of the Gallery of the Emanuel Art Center, loves putting on artistic boomerang shows. Neil's specialties include his 76 inch, larger than life sculpted boomerangs, ones that are fully functional. "But, you'd need to be the size of a giant to throw them," he said. "I do wall groupings, as well, including crucifixes with figurative elements on them."

He first became interested in boomerang art while teaching a three-dimensional design course, teaching basic sculpting techniques. Students were assigned to create one functional piece of art, whether it be a chair or a stereo cabinet.

"One student became interested in making a boomerang in 1979," Neil said. "He did research on how to make one, finding articles in a science publication, but then he never made the boomerang." Then, when Neil's daughter Leah gave him a foam boomerang in 1984, he remembered the student's research, and he pulled the science article from his files.

Now, he creates white sculpted boomerangs, in the vision of clouds and other abstract shapes. He also paints still life paintings, oil on canvas, using boomerangs as the subject matter, the boomerangs appearing to float in space.

Neil created a Siamese Air Foil Boomerang, with air foils on both the

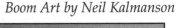

Boom Art by Neil Kalmanson

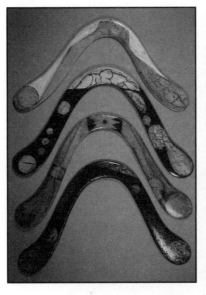

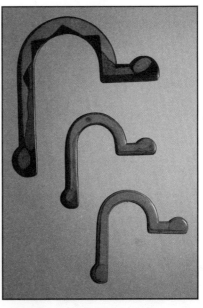

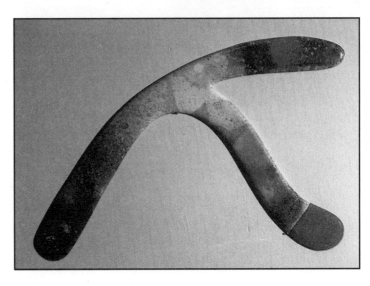

top and bottom, so you could turn the boomerang either way to throw it. He has described the Siamese Air Foil boom as one almost like two boomerangs glued together. While a typical boomerang has a flat side and a curved side, this boomerang curves on both the top and bottom. When you hold it with one side towards you, it flies low to the ground; flip it over and it soars then hovers back to you.

His boomerangs have been displayed in museums in New York, Mexico, Alabama, Florida and Georgia. They have won awards in the USBA categories of "best design," "best decorated," and "most innovative." An unusual, interlocking pair of his boomerangs have found a home in the Smithsonian Institute, and his boomerang that won the 1985 best aesthetics category now belongs to Ben Ruhe, the boomerang guru. "Ben has since added three more of my boomerangs to his collection," Neil said.

Kalmanson believes his 1987 boomerang show held at the Emanuel Arts Center was the first multi-artist show of its kind, featuring over 160 handcrafted boomerangs. The goal of the show was to "introduce the boomerang as a unique and valid vehicle for artistic expression."

In that show, fellow artist Patrick Cardiff presented boomerangs in the shapes of bats, barn owls, mermaids and mountain trout.

Kalmanson said the art of boomeranging fulfills his creative

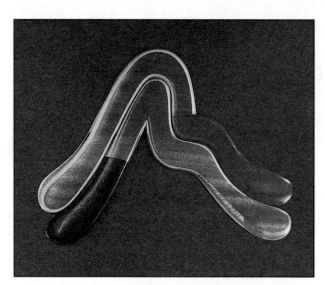

yearnings, while appealing to the scientific side of him, as well. He decorates the boomerangs with pastels and watercolors, colored pencils and inks, and oil based paints. Part of his creative mind must always be picturing what the completed boomerang will look like in flight.

He also uses a technique called decalcomania, which was first introduced in 1936 by surrealist painter Oscar Dominguez. He first saturates a textured material such as a wadded piece of a paper towel with ink, then he presses it onto a neutral colored boomerang. "This leaves a colored impression that has an element of surprise, and a character all its own."

He suggests approaching the project with a spirit of "playfulness and experimentation." He recommends trying a variety of textured material, including lace, burlap, and cloth. He also suggests using tangled yarn, rope and string, plastics and foils, sponges, crinkled tissue paper, rolled cardboard and anything else that appeals to your imagination.

"Aim for a balanced distribution of colors and textures," he said, adding that he usually keeps the tips of the boomerang white. "After a while, the images will begin to take on an identity of their own, and have a sense of completion."

If and when an ink blot suggests a landscape, figure or other image, he delineates them with a pen and black ink. "I prefer to draw quickly and loosely, using parallel lines to define negative areas. Concentrate, once again, on a balanced distribution of the negative areas, attempting to create interesting configurations. This kind of doodling, where your subconscious is doing the drawing, usually leads to a satisfying and often surprising abstract composition." He then covers the boomerang with a clear varnish.

Alan Scott Craig

Wanted: A Tall, Blonde, Boomerang Tossing Actor
What They Got: A Tall, Blonde Boomerang Tosser Who Says He Can't Act

"The field of boomerangs offer a special relationship between the individual and the environment. Experience this new art form and blend art, science, history and a relaxing form of meditation into one."
...Alan Scott Craig

Ceramic sculptor Alan Scott Craig was earning a living creating functional art pieces, like a vase with a vine in it that needed only infrequent watering. For a hobby and entertainment, he threw boomerangs.

Then, an acting call went out for the movie, The Bagdad Cafe, and former USA boomerang team member Jerry Caplan recommended Alan for the boom tossing part.

Alan Scott Craig
Wall Boom Art
Birds, Steer, Leopard

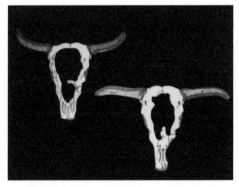

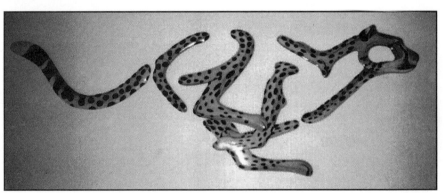

"I decided to throw a really artistic boomerang when I tried out for the part," Alan said, "so I created a functional toucan boomerang, painting it until 4 a.m. that morning. When the movie people showed up at my house at 9 a.m., the paint on the toucan had just dried."

The rest is history. Alan got the part, with reviews of the movie by Newsweek Magazine and The San Francisco Chronicle pointing out the "genius with a boomerang" and the "boomerang virtuoso."

Now, Alan has put aside his other forms of artistic endeavors, now creating only artistic boomerangs in his studio, appropriately renamed **The Art of Boomerang**. While he first made a basic V-shaped boomerang at the age of 12, he now creates exquisitely detailed boomerangs, often made into a set.

For example, he once created a wall hanging set of boomerangs, showing the story of an eagle catching a trout to take back to the nest. The first boomerang is in the shape of a small eagle, giving the impression of distance. As the eagle flies closer, each boomerang increases in size, angling to better see the face and talon-sharp feet.

The eagle dips, snatches a trout, circles around, the wings fully extended now. The trout panics as the eagle drops the fish into the nest. The final boomerang scene custom fits into the owner's mantelpiece, as the mother eagle fusses over her eaglets.

Another fascinating artistic design is made up of a pair of buffalo head boomerangs, with the negative space in the center creating the image of an American Indian in one, and an image of a bear in the other.

Negative space is the area of the boomerang that has been cut away; so, in Alan's boomerangs, even what technically does not exist turns into a beautiful art form.

And, for one of the most awesome boomerangs I've ever seen, Alan uses the negative space technique again, detailing a dramatic black, three boomeranged panther, a menacing look etched on his face. Then, in the center of the boomerang, in the part that is cut out, another catlike face appears. Then, between the legs of the cat, where again, the wood is cut away, a smaller catlike image peeks out.

He won first place honors at the 1988 USBA Nationals for the most creative design and for the most unusual shapes, while also snagging a first place finish in the competitive fast catch event in the 1988 California Corroboree. He won this event using his *African Secretary Bird* boomerang.

Panther

His boomerangs are also on display at the Air and Space Smithsonian Institute and are for sale at the Human Arts Gallery and the del Mano Gallery. All of his artistic wall hangings are made out of perfectly functioning, durably built boomerangs. "The vibrant colors that bring life to the boomerangs on the wall," Alan says, "also orchestrate a symphony of color through the air. Observers are attracted by the different silhouetted shapes that each boomerang projects against the sky."

Alan usually doesn't start a piece until he is commissioned to do so, because of the time involved. While one set of lion fish boomerangs took three months to actually create, for example, they took almost four years to conceptualize and design on paper.

But, that's okay; Alan doesn't mind. "I'm spending my lifetime," he said, "focusing on this very specific puzzle."

THE BOOMERANG
CAST INTO SPACE AND TIME
RETURNS
BECOMING WHAT WAS AND IS AGAIN
MAKES SOMETHING NEW
THAT NEVER WAS AND
MAKING IT DO
WHAT'S NEVER BEEN DONE
MERGING INTO SPACE AND TIME.
CAST INTO THE LOOKING-GLASS
IT RETURNS
WITH EINSTEIN AND ALICE
LEONARDO
AND NARCISSUS.

BEHOLD THE BOOMERANG'S FLIGHT
AS IT CIRCLES AND RETURNS
UPON ITSELF
AGAIN AND AGAIN
RECALLING ANCIENT SIGNS
FULL OF MEANING
AND MAGIC.

. . . Neil Kalmanson, poet

Women in Boomeranging:

Then and Now (Plus a Challenge!)

THEN:

It is a "well known and deplorable fact that fully nine-tenths of our girls and women are narrow chested and shoulder-bound. This is true because they have so little use for the muscles that throw the chest forward and shoulders back." ...*Things Worth Knowing about Brist, and Short Stories gleaned from historical research*, by the Brist Co., Topeka, Kansas, 1903.

NOW:

"Buzz! Wrong answer!"

...Michael Gel Girvin, world class boomerang thrower and boomerang instructor, in response to the 1903 quote.

Women have just as much potential to do well as both recreational and competitive throwers as men, given some arm strength and enough enthusiasm to stick with the sport.

...Betsylew Miale-Gix, 1996 International Women's Team Member, New Zealand, former world record holder, Aussie Round.

Betsylew Miale-Gix is fearless. She knows she can do it, and she just does it.

...Eric Darnell, world class boomerang pioneer.

Boomerang throwing is one of the few sports where women and men can compete side by side on a truly equal basis. I strongly object to shortening range requirements for women, and I strongly object to having separate men's and women's ratings. Since a ten-year old can make the twenty meter range, there's no point in even discussing special rules for women.

...Kelly Croman-Andretti, recreational boomerang competitor for ten years.

When I do boomerang demonstrations at schools, I draw a bullseye on the gym floor, and divide the classes into male and female teams. The children are supposed to throw the boomerang so it will land inside the bullseye. Ninety percent of the time, the girls beat the boys — they just have more finesse.

...Gary Broadbent, world record holder, member of the 1996 USA *Team 1*, New Zealand.

Boomerang throwing is skill over power, and that puts the sexes on very equal footing. Height and weight have very little to do with success. Men and women, equal terms.

...Chet Snouffer, 1994 World/10 time US Champion.

When I did a demonstration in Hawaii, the girls did just as well as the boys in the fast catch race. Many of the boys just go nuts, throwing too hard, while the girls flipped the boomerang correctly.

...John Flynn, 1995 US Nationals Champion.

Women have been involved in some of the most interesting chapters of my flying life. My first instructor in powered airplanes was a woman. A woman taught me how to fly Pitts specials. A woman soloed me in hot air balloons. Some of the best hang glider pilots are women. Now, a woman has taught me how to throw boomerangs.

...Dan Neelands, pilot and recreational boomerang thrower.

I believe that if more women knew about boomerang throwing, they'd get involved, too.

...Vera Broadbent, 1995 Waki Klak National Kylie Champion, placing 4th overall in the 1995 Open Division Nationals, and earning a first place in trick catch.

"Is twenty-seven a good score?"

...Carmen Snouffer, first place in accuracy in 1986 nationals, member of victorious Team Midwest in 1987 International Competition.

Carmen Snouffer

That last quote may need a little explaining. In the days when nine-tenths of the women were narrow chested and shoulder bound, the wife of Chet Snouffer would have sat demurely on the sidelines, clapping sweetly for her man. While Carmen certainly cheers Chet on every chance she gets, she also beat everyone in the accuracy event, including Chet, earning 27 out of 30 possible points, during the 1986 US National Boomerang Competition.

Chet points out that when Carmen won the accuracy event, it was a more difficult event, "when you didn't have slots and holes and flaps to help you out. You threw the boom and tried to get it right back."

Carmen was the first female member of an international team in 1987, competing on the victorious *Team Midwest*. She competed in Australian Round and Accuracy, with her team sweeping those events. She served as USBA President in 1986 and 1987.

Obviously, a woman can throw a boomerang. Why, then, are so few of the champions female?

"With girls , we have a problem because without more local adult females available for them to adopt as role models, we aren't going to get as many to stick with it after the initial fun stuff is over," Betsylew Miale-Gix said. "Some parents are not gender-neutral in their parenting and still point boys towards sporting activities, assertiveness, taking chances even at possible physical risk, but don't impart the same orientation to their girls."

Chet Snouffer believes social roles have prevented too many women from throwing. "Until twenty years ago, there weren't many women's teams in ball sports. Now, girls grow up throwing and kicking and playing ball, and as time goes on, more and more girls will throw boomerangs. Booms give us a chance to compete across a broad spectrum, with fifteen-year olds competing with forty-two year old adults, and either one has a good chance of winning."

Beside being a cultural thing, boomerang throwing also appears to be a couple thing. The small number of women seriously involved in boomerang throwing seem to do so with a husband or boyfriend.

Kelly Croman-Andretti taught her pilot boyfriend Dan Neelands how to throw boomerangs, and now they throw together on beaches all over the country. Carmen started tossing after she met husband Chet, when they taught gymnastics classes together. Vera learned to throw while dating now husband Gary, and she competed in the 1994 International Competition, held in Japan. Betsylew competes and practices with her husband, Will Gix, who stepped in for the injured Mike Dickson in New Zealand.

Michael Gel Girvin wants to encourage women in the sport. "Historically, in the sport of boomeranging, men and women, the few women that have competed, have competed on even ground. Even in the power events, such as Fast Catch, Endurance, MTA and Distance, women have always done well. Betsylew has dominated in Fast Catch and Endurance over the years, and Callie Laurent used to excel in the Distance event. There is absolutely no reason why women can't be every bit as good as men throwers in this sport."

Girvin is adamant: "When I work with children, the girls have been as good as the boys. They just have to be taught athletics from an early age, and encouraged! To make a parallel, someday soon, there will probably be a woman who makes it in Major League Baseball. Why? Because unlike thirty years ago, little girls are playing in Little League. They are being encouraged from an early age to become athletic. And, sooner or later, a woman will make it."

"A lot of women never really learned to pitch a softball or other skills that might make learning to throw boomerangs simpler," said Kelly Croman-Andretti. "Learning to throw may be initially harder for many women because it doesn't come as naturally."

THE CHALLENGE:

It's time to correct the wrong answer. Women and girls from the East Coast, West Coast, Any Coast, Midwest, Southwest, South, North and anywhere in between - why don't you become one of the all-too-small number of female throwers, the ones with the confidence, the strength and the passion to throw and catch as good as the guys?

E- mail me at Dark Print@aol.com with all your success stories. I know they'll be coming! Matter of fact, I'll go check my mail box now. . .

I'VE COME A LONG WAY FROM CHRISTMAS
OF EIGHTY-TWO
WITH TWO HUNDRED BOOMS
AND SOME SKILL DID ENSUE.
SO, HOW DID YOU GET STARTED IN BOOMS
- AND BE FRANK!
AS FOR ME, I HAVE MY MOTHER TO THANK.

Bud Pell, recreational boomerang thrower and poet, who received
his first boomerang from his Mom when he was 49 years old.

Betsylew Miale-Gix

Brier, Washington

"Becoming a boomerang artist goes hand in hand with becoming entranced by the mystery and beauty of boomerangs in flight, the link between throwing and nature, the cultural heritage and roots of throwing in early aboriginal peoples. It isn't that there is any boomerang movement bias against women designing or decorating boomerangs. Rather, there aren't enough women involved who also have the requisite artistic talent and/or woodworking/engineering talent and desire to make and decorate boomerangs."...Betsylew Miale-Gix

While Betsylew has intriguing thoughts about the qualifications of boomerang artists, she isn't one herself. Instead, she's an athlete and a competitor, often the only female tossing boomerangs in a field full of men.

Betsylew Miale-Gix

It would be dangerous to let your guard down around her, however, expecting a female to need a handicap like in some sports. During the 1995 season, she was fifth out of all United States throwers in both Fast Catch and Endurance. Betsylew also scored a 40 out of 50 possible points in the Accuracy Event in the World Championships in New Zealand, tying with two German throwers for first place.

"They both agreed with me not to have a throw off," she said. "Why should any one of us have to feel like a loser after doing so well? Besides, it was in the proper spirit of international goodwill and sportsmanship to share the title."

She competed on the International Women's team, a group of women gathered from the United States, Germany and France. She threw in 14 of the 15 events, competing against the teams of men from around the globe.

Her team beat the New Zealand team, and they were ahead of another team until the last day of events. At the New Zealand International Individual Championship Tournament, Betsylew finished as the 42nd highest ranked thrower in the world today.

"I have a history of playing competitive team sports like softball and basketball, and individual sports like tennis and badminton," Betsylew said. "Even so, one of the main reasons I began throwing, then became a serious thrower and activist in the boom community was my relationship with my husband Will."

"I'm more intensively competitive than Will, but throwing well and succeeding is also important to him," said Betsylew, "Over the years, we have evolved to a good comfort level with the fact that we are trying to outdo one another, even in practice."

She admits that it can be difficult when one spouse throws much better than the other in a tournament. "While we're always rooting for the other to do well, we can occasionally sulk if it goes great for one and lousy for the other, but we get over it quickly."

"Though, to be honest," she added, "this was not always the case. We have mellowed in the last few years."

She believes that their friendly competing is usually helpful. "We don't want to be consistently outdone by the other, even when we practice."

Once, when the couple competed in the Salem Oregon Tournament a few years ago, Betsylew and Will were both up for the MTA throw at the same time. Now, you remember Will, the guy who held the Australian Round world record for about ten seconds before Mark Weary set a new world record?

Apparently, the winds of coincidence know just how to find Will. After a solid flight, he and Betsylew both caught their MTA boomerangs. "What was Betsylew's time?" 29.81 seconds.

"Okay, what was Will's time?" 29.81 seconds.

While in New Zealand, she and her husband enjoyed both the competition and a nine-and-a-half day trip in a camper van throughout the paradise of the country. She describes it this way. "We got to see the south island, hike the hills, mountains and forests, and see the valleys full of sheep, domestic deer or cattle, and farms, lakes, rivers and diverse coastlines of the east, south and west."

"We walked to glaciers, along lakes, through subtropical rainforests, temperate rainforests and temperate forests, on black, grey or white sandy beaches, rocky beaches, fantastic mountains, canyons and gorges, viewing wildlife and birds from yellow-eyed and little blue penguins to royal albatross, Australian Harriers, New Zealand hawks, brown teal, white faced herons, bellbirds, pukekos, fantails, tui, yellow crowned parakeets, flightless birds like the Weka, to seals."

"It was a nature buff, bird watcher, hikers' paradise," she added, "perfectly suited to Will and me."

Now that the couple is settled back again in the United States, it's time for more practice. Betsylew gifted her husband Will with a boom nickname, " Showdog, " while Michael Gel Girvin nicknamed him "Smooth as Silk." She, however, has no nickname. "Odd, but true," she said. "Perhaps this is a reflection of my unique-for-now status as the only high-level female competitor."

The couple had just thrown for the same event, at the same time, both catching inside the circle, both with the exact same time, down to the hundredth of a second!

She wishes more women would become involved in the sport. "We need to entice more women with athletic ability and strong arms," she said. "The person who has played a throwing sport like softball is the most obvious fit. They have much of the throwing motion in muscle memory already, and the hand-eye coordination necessary for successful catching."

Betsylew admits that it is a frustrating process taking the time to become competent at boomerangs, if you're used to being good at the other sports you play. "While there are skill overlaps, things like direction to the wind, tuning, adjusting throw height, power and angle at release all must be learned from scratch over time."

She believes having others to practice with, learn from and to socialize with are important for success. "With tournaments to go to, throwers can be inspired by throwing with those of greater skill and gain rewards for the degree of skill the newer thrower has already attained."

"I don't think that continuing athletic achievement as adults is as important to women's sense of self worth and personal well being as it is for men," she added. "Perhaps this will change in future generations as more and more young women are competing in sports both in and out of school."

She also believes that it will be difficult to recruit young women with strong throwing arms, good hand/eye coordination and quickness and agility, because those women will tend to focus on the sports that can get them a college scholarship, an Olympic opportunity and/or professional income producing futures, mainly volleyball, softball, tennis and basketball.

On the other hand, she likes the fact that boomerang tournaments do not offer cash prizes. "I have advocated preserving this as the status quo until we're in a position to have noncompetitor officials and scorekeepers."

"I believe it would threaten the camaraderie, sportsmanship and trust we have in one another as thrower's who also officiate for each other at tournaments," she said, "if a thrower's line call or count of catches, or decision on whether the trick catch was good or not, could mean the differences between that thrower winning money or not."

She points out the tradition of cheering for each other at competitions, even if by doing well, the other thrower will beat some of those cheering. She believes that this could fade, if cash prizes were involved.

Betsylew is fascinated by how boomerangs are made, what makes them work, and how they fly. "Despite all that," she added, "when it comes time around our house for someone to go out into

Betsylew believes that many women have "less inclination to use the comparatively smaller amount of leisure time our lives afford us for serious athletic practice and competition."

the garage and design, outline, cut and sand new sticks, Will does the work, not me."

Instead, she enjoys checking air foils and discussing design issues, such as whether or not to add holes, test-flying booms, correcting boomerang design problems and deciding how to decorate them.

One of her biggest contributions to the boomerang world, however, is that of the **Toss Across America**, with the sixth annual event held on May 18, 1996. The *Toss Across America* consists of several simultaneous teaching and demonstration events hosted by USBA throwers in their own communities designed to introduce boomerang throwing to new throwers countrywide.

She offers each participating group hints for organizing their *Toss Across America* event, along with a large color poster for publicity, an official press release, and USBA information sheets.

Booming Around the World

While the American boomerangers are certainly competitive powerhouses, outstanding crafts people and artists, and technological geniuses, extraordinary boomerang experts also live all around the planet. While it would be impossible to mention them all, here is a quick glimpse of a few of those people.

First, **Rob Croll** of Australia. Rob certainly has had an impressive twenty-two year career in boomeranging, holding almost every Australian throwing record at one time or another, including the still current Australian record of 765 consecutive catches, and a brand new endurance round record of 59.

He also still holds his country's trick catching record of 27, along with Australia's MTA record, with a time of 2 minutes, 33 seconds. He set the record for the return of the world's smallest boomerang, as well, tossing a boom only 5 by 5 centimeters out 20 meters, with a successful return.

Rob served well on the Australian team that challenged the Americans in 1981, travelling to all three spots in Australia, in order to compete in all three matches.

He remembers that first occasion well, laughing about his expectations about the Americans. "I figured we were the experts, and the Americans were the tourists, here to learn about throwing," he said. "My stomach, though, did a backflip when I first saw Chet Snouffer somersaulting around, throwing his boomerangs. I thought - *Crikey*! What on earth is going on here?"

Rob and Chet competed hard against each other then, and again in 1988 and 1989, when the two met in international competitions.

Rob won the World Champion title in 1988, while he placed second in the 1989 World Cup, behind Chet. By 1991, however, Rob dropped to 14th place in the world tourney in Perth, and in the world cup in Germany in 1992, he'd fallen even further, down to 40th place.

He didn't even attend the world championships in Japan in 1994, and in New Zealand, his team ran into plenty of difficulties, landing in 10th place. There were even whispers about "the death of a legend."

"I was pretty bummed," Rob admitted. "We'd had incredible luck with the wind, all bad, and to boot, we threw badly, too." The New Zealand individual tournaments weren't going to start until the next day, so, just for fun, just to pass the time of day, the world class competitors decided to hold a Suicide Competition. It meant absolutely nothing, nothing at all.

About 80 throwers lined up, shoulder to shoulder, and they began throwing. In "Suicide," once you drop a boomerang, you're out of the competition. Eventually, there were only about five or six people on the field, all still tossing and catching their boomerangs at the same time. "There were a couple of young Australians, plus Gary Broadbent and me," Rob said, with a laugh. "There was no way I wanted any of them to beat me, so I kept going."

The other Australians dropped a boom. Rob and Gary, his house guest for the week, kept tossing. And tossing. Then, Rob won.

American Barnaby Ruhe flung Rob onto his shoulders, and raced him around the field, amidst clapping and cheers.

" I always say," Rob added, " if the throws don't really count, I can always do well."

The next day, Rob returned for the individual championships. "It was a magic moment," Barnaby Ruhe said. "it was great seeing Robbie Croll re-realize - hey, I'm Robbie Croll and I can take this thing." Rob agrees that he felt much better after the Suicide event. "It was quite a bit of a turnaround, after a shockingly bad week."

And, although the competition was tight, with Americans Steve Kavanaugh, Mark Weary and Chet Snouffer in close contention, Rob Croll went on to be the 1996 World Champion.

Again. Eight years after he once held the world title, four years after placing 40th in Germany, and two years after he didn't even compete at all in Japan, Rob Croll is once again the World Champion boomerang thrower.

Now, on to **Yannick Charles**, the French National Champion in 1993, 1994 and 1995. Yannick holds three world records, and in 1996, he planned to beat two of his very own records.

First, juggling. Chet Snouffer held the world juggling record of 502 until Yannick recently tossed an amazing 555 juggling booms in a row.

In juggling, the competitor must toss out a boomerang, then throw out a second one before catching the first. One boomerang must always be in motion during this event, and the thrower's total score equals the number of booms tossed before he or she drops or misses one.

Juggling was an official tournament event until 1994, but Yannick still plans to toss it again this year. "I hope to have a record of more than 600 this year," Yannick said. "That's one of my goals."

Yannick also co-holds the world endurance record, where a thrower must toss and catch as many boomerangs as possible in a five minute time period, with each boom flying out at least twenty meters. The record? An amazing 76!

And, what does Yannick think of his record? "I think it will be beaten more than once in 1996," he said. "I hope to receive a score of at least 80 in endurance this year."

Yannick holds still another incredible record, earning the world record in consecutive catches. How many do you think Yannick tossed and caught in a row? At least 555. What about 750? Maybe even 1000?

Try *one thousand, two hundred and fifty one* catches.

Yannick practices daily. " I'm very happy when I'm throwing, " he said. "It's still like magic to me. If I don't throw even one day, I really miss it."

He was off to another great year in 1996. Winning the first French tournament of the year, he's looking forward to working towards another national title. "I think I can do it because I really enjoy what I'm doing," he said. "I want to be perfect, so I keep trying, and I won't give up." And, if he's right about records soon to be broken, 1997-1998 should be another great year.

Disappointed with his New Zealand performance, he said he can't be happy when he performs less than his best. "I ended up 24th in New Zealand, and I know I could have done better," he said. "After the first two events, I figured I couldn't win, so maybe I quit trying so hard then."

Yannick makes all of his own boomerangs. "I only throw my own," he said. "I think it's better if you throw something you made yourself."

As Yannick prepares for the season ahead of him, he mentions one more important item to remember. "You need to get a lot of pleasure out of boomerang throwing. That's a goal, just like trying to set a world record is a goal."

While Yannick said there are between 400 and 500 boomerang throwers in his country, other countries are still struggling to build interest in the sport. For example, Canada. Thrower **Eric Promislow** describes the general Canadian attitude towards the returning stick as "benign interest."

"When most people see me throw, there is a shrug of the shoulder, a live and let live kind of thing," Eric said. "There are few throwers here, and we look to Americans like Gary Broadbent, Chet Snouffer and Michael Gel Girvin for boomerang enthusiasm."

Canadians did field a 1994 International team in Japan, tying for 7th place out of 10 spots. "One guy, however, was a novice, and another man lived in America, although he had Canadian roots. We made up 150 t-shirts, and we gave away as many as we sold," Promislow said.

Eric started out as a juggler, but became frustrated when he reached a tough plateau. Then, he turned to boomerang throwing. "For me, competing is an important part of growing in a sport, and with juggling, there wasn't the competition; the atmosphere was too laid back."

Stephane Marguerite, also a Canadian, achieved 801 consecutive catches in 1989, and he is the driving force behind Canada's only boomerang club, *The Montreal Boomerang Club.*

The Captain of the Canadian boomerang team, he teaches boom tossing in the park on Saturday afternoons, and he puts on demon-

Rob Croll
Australia

Yannick Charles
France

Stephane Marguerite
Eric Promislow
Canada

Harri Pietila
Heikki Niskanen
Finland

Fridolin Frost
Germany

strations, workshops and competitions to follow through on the club's aim of promoting "the sport of boomerangs on Montreal, in the province of Quebec and beyond."

In Finland, thrower **Harri Pietila** is also struggling to form a boomerang club. "I've only found about 8 people who have thrown a boomerang, and are interested in the sport," he said. "But, plans are to have the first competition this year, and I'll try to write a newsletter soon."

"Some of our throwers have gotten boomerangs while on holiday in Australia, some made them themselves, and others purchased them from Americans, like the Boomerang Man," he added. "Others get information via e-mail."

The first planned competition was the *Arctic Midnight Sun Boomerang Competition*, held on June 21, 1996. **Heikki Niskanen** from the Department of Applied Tetrapiloktomy at the University of Kuopio was involved with the competition, and he plans to maintain a web page about the event at: http://www.uku.fi/hniskane/sunboom.html

It must have been an awesome day, with rangs tossed at the connecting point of Finland, Sweden and Norway. His boomerang association, the **AFKD** is stationed in Kuopio, Finland, but they have members from Sweden, Estonia, Switzerland, Spain, Russia, Georgia, Australia and the United States. "Activity is not very high, but still intensive," Heikki said.

And, finally, what would this chapter be like without a word from the 1996 world championship team, the Germans?

Now, lots of people own boomerangs. Some people wear boomerang jewelry, style their hair with boomerang shaped hairbrushes and decorate their homes with exquisite boomerang art.

But, **Fridolin Frost** of the winning *Young Guns* German boomerang team is probably the only boom enthusiast with a boomerang shaped collarbone.

Fridolin was competing on the International boomerang team in the world tournament held in Japan. After he scored a second place finish in fast catch there, and his teammate, American Gary Broadbent snagged the first place spot, the two men leaped up to slap each other with a high five.

Great throwing; bad fall. Fridolin lost his balance, and broke his collarbone, and it healed in a boomerang shape. The boombone doesn't appear to have hurt the world class thrower's skillful boom chucking, however. Fridolin, the 1992 World Champion, set the German and European Aussie Round record in 1995, scoring an amazing 90 points.

Add that record to his world record MTA limited of 1 minute and 24 seconds, and his German juggling record of 353.

"I'd take Fridolin on my team any day," Gary Broadbent said. "You're only as strong as your weakest link, and Fridolin has no weaknesses. He's the German Chet Snouffer."

A Note on Virginia Beach, 1996

Hosted by 1991 World Champ John Koehler

Some of the most awesomely powerful boom tossers of the country banded together in Virginia Beach for the 1996 Boomerang National Tournament. Eyewitnesses there say that when Chet Snouffer arrived, he was already focused on winning that coveted title, one that he'd already held *nine* times before. Chet stood back a little bit, surveying the fields and all that was around them. When brother Gregg Snouffer called him "The Dinosaur of Delaware," Chet just smiled.

He knew that, while dinosaurs were certainly not young anymore, dinosaurs were still the most powerful creatures ever to roam the earth. And, so it happened.

Chet Snouffer, The Dinosaur of Delaware, became the National Champion for the incredible 10th, emphasize this - for the *tenth* time. While many boom throwers would give away their most highly prized rangs for just one shot at the title, Chet had just accumulated one full decades worth.

"Just think," Chet observed, "when I first won the title, Adam Ruhf was just six years old!"

To win the National Title once is an accomplishment revered among rang-ers; to win it ten times is to create a legend and achieve immortality. Chet Snouffer, Champion.

As if that wasn't enough, that isn't all that happened in Virginia Beach. Adam Ruhf, sixteen years old, having announced just two weeks before the event that he was going after an almost untouchable world record, the 76 catches in Endurance, a record held by Yannick Charles of France, went out and made 76 catches. He tied the world record. Eyewitness accounts vary on whether Adam dropped one or two boomerangs during that event, but all agree that his performance approached absolute perfection.

As if to provide a backdrop of mythical proportion to the competitions there in Virginia Beach, by enormous coincidence, the first three letters of the Radisson Hotel sign were burned out giving visible emphasis to what was taking place on the fields of competition. Yes, what happened at Virginia Beach in 1996 was truly R-A-D!!

Boomeranging Resources

Finding quality boomerang resources can be similar to the circular flight of the boomerang itself. When world class thrower Gary Broadbent checked the computer at his local library for boomerang leads, he was thrilled to see a category called: boomerang - experts.

Excited, he clicked on it, only to read: experts - see Gary Broadbent.

There are, however, excellent newsletters, Internet resources and boomerang manufacturers/teachers to be found. Here are the some of the best:

One is the official newsletter of the United States Boomerang Association (USBA), called **Many Happy Returns**.

The **USBA** is a non-profit organization whose goal is to promote the art, craft, sport and poetry of boomeranging through events, competitions and information distributed through the quarterly newsletter.

The address of the U.S. Boomerang Association is P.O. Box 182, Delaware, Ohio 43015. Their fax number is 1-614-363-4414, and the email address of the secretary, Gregg Snouffer is 75574.2346@compuserve.com

The organization elects officers, including a president, vice president, secretary, treasurer and a five member board of directors. Membership dues are $15 per year, with a lifetime membership costing $225. The Canadian lifetime membership is $250.

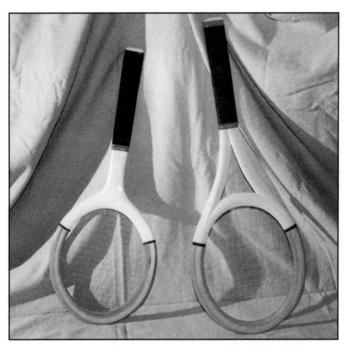

Tennis Racket Booms by Bob Letzin

A typical issue contains the USBA Buzz column, information about tournaments, boomerang contests and letters to the editor, each letter with a personal answer directly below it.

There are columns that describe throwing techniques and reviews of boomerang products, including plans on how to build a boomerang.

The USBA store lists various boomerang products to buy, including the official USBA competition rulebook, USBA t-shirts and articles on boomerang throwing.

It includes boomerang comics, a list of boomerang throwers' e-mail addresses, competition photos and news and lists of boomerang clubs, organizations and manufacturers.

Another terrific boomerang publication is **Boomerang News**, a newsletter by Ted Bailey. Produced 10 times a year, each issue has eight pages of boomerang scoop, including plenty of international information. The newsletter costs $10 a year in the United States or Canada, and $20 overseas. The address is Ted Bailey, Boomerang News, P.O. Box 6076 - Ann Arbor, MI 48106.

This newsletter also provides plenty of boomerang photos, along with addresses and phone numbers of throwers around the world. In the March, 1996 issue, for example, there is a photo of an early gum trading card, with an American Indian holding a rabbit stick called a "Putch-Kohu."

The main article in that issue is about a true returning aboriginal boomerang owned by General Douglas MacArthur. After the general escaped from the Japanese invasion of the Phillipines, he set up headquarters in Australia. There, the Australian officers presented him with a boomerang on his 63rd birthday on January 26, 1943.

All 26 of the Australian officers signed the boomerang, making it one of the earliest known signed boomerangs. The inscription reads, "To General Douglas MacArthur C in C, S.W.P.A. - A small token from the Australian Officers - G.H.O. on your birthday 26 Jan. 1943 - "Australia Day."

Ted's newsletter also includes lighter boomerang moments, such as a cartoon portraying five throw stick carrying cavemen running for their lives from a fierce, hungry looking Tyrannosaurus Rex. One cave man shouts, *I said NO TEST SHOTS!!!*"

Ted also puts out an amazingly complete booklet of boomerang resources, listing boomerang manufacturers, including names, addresses, phone numbers, email addresses and their specialties. He includes information on boomerang clubs and organizations, both in the US and overseas, along with places to buy boomerang construction materials. Incredible stuff.

He sells the regularly updated list for $3 for non-subscribers to Boomerang News, and for $2 for subscribers. It's well worth the money, immediately providing names, addresses, email addresses and phone numbers of the best connections in the boomerang world today. He also includes a paragraph for each, listing the specialties of each boom resource person.

He also sells collections of previous boomerang newsletters for $40 to $50, and various boomerang text files, database collections and boomerang flight simulations, all on disk. There are plenty of articles, photos and statistics in these that any true boom enthusiastic would love to own. The boom lists, the disks and the newsletters can be purchased at the same address as the Boomerang News.

Ted suggests contacting him for the latest subscription information, and a listing of currently available information services.

NEWSLETTERS

Yet a third newsletter is the **Boomerang Competition Update**: Connecting Boomerang Throwers Coast to Coast by Chicago Bob. This publication is called the ultimate periodical for the competing athlete. It provides you with up to date tournament results, USBA rankings and all the necessary news about serious competition. The subscription costs $10 for 6 issues, with the publication coming out monthly during the competition season.

If there are tournaments during seven months of the year, though, Bob puts out that extra issue, including it in the regular subscription cost.

And, if someone subscribes during the summer, for example, Chicago Bob would forward every issue printed so far for the season.

In the final issue each year, he lists the entire ratings system for all USBA competitions throughout that season. He provides the names of all event winners for the year, and he highlights the top ten on the cover to point out their special achievements.

He provides detailed information about the scores received in the major tournaments for the year, as well. "Presently, this is the only place to see the entire National Ratings," Bob added. The address for the newsletter is: Chicago Bob, Boomerang Competition Update, P.O. Box 242, Waterloo, IL 62298.

And, if you speak German, Gerhardt Bertling edits a newsletter called "**Bumerang Welt,**" translated as Boomerang World. In that newsletter, they focus on archaeological discoveries, the physics of boomerangs and plans for making boomerangs, including new tools to use and the decoration of the rangs.

They rarely report tournament results, although they do explain the tournament events for beginning throwers.

Gerhardt said the German viewpoint of boomerangs is a little different than the American one. While many United States throwers don't make their own boomerangs, many Germans make boomerangs but don't compete.

" Many throwers only use the element 'sport', " Gerhardt said. " Most of the German throwers make their own boomerangs, and in Germany we have a lot of boomerang enthusiasts who don't take part in competitions. They only make and throw boomerangs for fun and their main element is making rangs."

He personally names three elements of boomeranging that he finds fascinating. "I make boomerangs, nice ones like my strip laminated models and competition rangs that I use myself. I also compete in tournaments and I throw as often as I can. And, I like to think about the physics - why does it come back?"

To subscribe to Bumerang Welt, you need to send a check or money order in DM. The cost is 26. - DM for four issues, and the subscription address is: Bumerang-Verlag, Postfach 3230, 22825 Norderstedt, Germany. Put your request to the attention of Wilhelm Bretfeld.

And, if you join the *Club de boomerang de Montreal*, you'll receive their bulletin, "**Distance**." The cost for club membership, including the newsletter, is $15 annually. This club, run by Canadian Boomerang Team member Stephane Marguerite, aims to "promote the sport of boomerangs in Montreal, in the province of Quebec, and beyond."

Their newsletter contains information about the worldwide boomeranging scene. Send your check or money order to 4545 Pierre-De Coubertin, Montreal (Quebec) HIV 3R2.

INFO SOURCES

Okay, back to the States. Tom Fisher, owner of Greyford Co. Boomerangs, has offered to answer any questions about the sport. He sells boomerangs made by Michael Girvin and Doug DuFresne, while offering three of his own creations. "I'm open to any questions people may have about their boomerangs," he said. "I welcome newcomers especially." His address is: Tom Risher, PO Box 4734, Whittler, CA 90607.

For more details about boomerang publications and information, contact Tony Brazelton at 2405 Lawndale Drive, Champaign, IL 61821. "I have much info at my disposal which I can e-mail to people in answer to nearly any question about boomerangs," Tony said, "or I can point them to sources available in their library."

Tony has been throwing for thirteen years now, starting when he was age ten. He holds free lessons every nice weather Sunday for neighborhood kids and other residents, and he also does boomerang demonstrations for schools and clubs.

1992 was a big year for Tony, because he started competing then, and he also formed the *Illini Boomerang Club* on the University of Illinois campus. "We soon noticed a mysterious $50 in our treasury," he said. "It was left over from an earlier boomerang club in the 1980s, formed by Paul Sprague."

And, while Tony hopes to resurrect his club when he isn't quite so busy working on his graduate degree in neuroscience, Paul Sprague has already created a new club, that of the *Wandering Nutmegs*.

And, the Wandering Nutmeg Boomerang Club has a mission: to teach the entire state of Connecticut how to throw a boomerang, one person at a time.

The unusual name combines the club's wandering around the state to perform boomerang feats with Connecticut's nickname of the nutmeg state. The club formed in 1990, and has a core group of members who keep training and encouraging their mailing list group of about 250 people. Their crowning moment was when Moleman set an Aussie Round record during one of their tournaments.

Their spokesperson, Paul Sprague, usually ranks between 20th and 30th in the nation. "I'm not a super-serious competitor," he said. "My main goal is to bring new people into the sport and to introduce them to how boomerangs work."

To contact the club, call Paul Sprague at 1-203-245-8211.

And, for a complete boomerang catalogue, probably one of the longest running boom places in America today, contact the *Boomerang Man*, Rich Harrison himself. The Boomerang Man sells products from throwers and manufacturers ranging from Chet Snouffer in Ohio to Michael Gel Girvin in California. Rich started a newsletter, the **News-O-Rang** in 1976, the first known American boomerang newsletter. He created three issues, making those newsletters collectors items in themselves. The News-O-Rang was an early form of boom networking, with Rich offering the following advice: He believes that 99 percent of all boomerang breakages resulted from a malfunction of the throwing apparatus - in other words, you. "You didn't compute properly," Rich said. "Boomerangs will only do what you program into it."

"I was happy when Ben Ruhe started the *Many Happy Returns* newsletter, and I'm really pleased that Ted Bailey continues his wonderful efforts," Rich said.

He laughs about being introduced as the Boomerang Man. "I feel like people expect me to change into a costume in a burst of lightning," he said.

He specializes in matching boomerangs with the level of experience of the thrower. "Most people appreciate that," he said, "so they aren't spending half of their time getting it out the tree."

To contact the Boomerang Man, call him at 1-318-325-8157, or email him at bmanrich@iamerica.net or write to 1806 North 3rd Street, Monroe, LA 71201. His fax number is 1-318-329-1095. He accepts VISA, MASTERCARD and Discover Card.

"Overseas buyers will find credit cards the fastest method of payment," Rich said. "I also advise people who order through e-mail to include their snailmail address and phone number when writing or ordering."

He provides a free catalogue, with a 1-800 number provided for orders. He includes detailed throwing instructions with each purchase. Also, if you provide him with an e-mail address or a fax number, he will send you up to date boomerang news, as it happens.

And, while Bud Pell was extraordinarily generous in sharing his boom poetry here, there is still more available. To order Bud's complete book of poetry, called **Bud's Boomerhymes, Odes, and Ballads,** send $5 to Bud Pell. This price includes postage; the address is 33047 Chapman Circle, Westland, Michigan 48185.

Bud is a terrific inspiration for those of us who aren't still fifteen years old. His mother gifted him with his first boomerangs in 1982, when he was 49 years old. Six years later, at the age of 55, he started competing in tournaments.

For a fascinating visual look at boomerangs, check out Graham Coates of South Australia's new CD, "**Boomerang: Echoes of Australia.**" The CD includes movies on how to throw boomerangs. While ordering information is incomplete at this time, the *Boomerang Man* can be contacted for further details.

And, in order to show a broader spectrum of the boomerang prism, I couldn't delve too deeply into any one subject. For those of you who want more information on specific topics, here are a few resources:

For more boom slang, or to get to know individual throwers in any more depth, the best solution is to head to the nearest boomerang event.

For those of you that are intrigued by the absolute latest word on boom construction, respected boomerang crafter Dr. Fredric Malmberg has recently completed a book, one that he calls a "builders manual rather than a glossy hardback or coffee table type book."

The book includes chapters on simple plywood model construction, but it concentrates on lap joint construction. He is including numerous construction drawings, to allow even novices to build booms.

He will list throwing instructions, tuning instructions and information on how to build a competition style boomerang. While he was in the process of contacting printers at the time of our book's publication, he suggests that you contact him for further information. He expects the price to be less than $20.

You can write to Fredric A. Malmberg, DPM, 1545 East Market Street, York, PA 17403. Or, email him at fmalmb@Mem.po.com or call him at 1-717-848-4601.

To contact Alan Scott Craig about his artistic boomerangs, you can contact him at 358 Bard Street, Fillmore, California 93015, or by calling him at 1-805-524-2045.

To get more information about Neil Kalmanson's artistic work, you can write to him at 766 Old Nunez Road, Swainsboro, Georgia, 30401.

INTERNET

Web sites and e-mail:
75574.2346@compuserve.com

majordomo@jcn.com

michaelg@im4u.net

thrower-request@dfw.net

plantspeak@aol.com

darkprint@aol.com

chibob@ns.htc.net

http://staff.uiuc.edu/~brazelto/
USBAinfo.html

tbailey@ic.net

Please contact author for
updates on resources, Website
and e-mail addresses change.

And now, boom cyberspace.

For a terrific place on the Internet to exchange messages with boomerang addicts across the world, go to the newsgroup alt. boomerang. There, you'll find throwers debating the merits of various boomerangs, discussing the role of women in the throwing world and disagreeing about the validity of competition rules, while still finding time to chat about the awesome tosses of the day.

America On-Line users should type in keyword newsgroup, and follow the directions to select alt.boomerang.   For Compuserve, type Go Internet, select Usenet Newsgroups, then follow screen directions. For Prodigy, use the Jump command to Usenet, then follow further instructions.

Another alternative is to subscribe to majordomo@jcn.com. If interested in joining this group, email that address, with the words: subscribe rang-list end

Each time a subscriber mails a message to that e-mail address, every other subscriber gets a copy. Any questions about this new service should be directed to Michael Gray at michaelg@im4u.net

The service started on March 6, 1996 and 80 subscribers signed up during the first thirty days, 100 people by the end of six weeks. Subscribers are from the United States, Canada, Mexico, Dominican Republic, Sweden, Finland, Norway, The Netherlands, Germany, Slovenia, Italy, Belgium, Scotland, England, Japan, Australia and France.

Gray said new subscribers are signing up every day, and he expects the list to be most active during warm weather. Common topics on this mailing list include upcoming tournaments and recently completed tournaments, techniques for making and painting boomerangs and finding people to throw with in a certain geographical area.

I joined the service by asking for information to use in this book. That very same day, I got a message - from myself, of course, asking for information for this book.

Hey the sending and receiving of my message - - that's almost like the circular flight of —

No, I won't say it. I just can't. Neither my husband nor my editor can stand one more boomerang pun. You'll just have to finish that sentence yourself. I hope you understand.

Another Internet service is called *Thrower*. To subscribe, send the following message - "subscribe thrower" to thrower-request@dfw.net. The subject matter of this service is much broader, with members talking about throw sticks and bolos, as well. Since I've subscribed to the service, I've read little discussion specifically targeted to boomerang throwers, but Ted Bailey recommends their web page, calling the boomerang section "absolutely top rate." The

Thrower WWW page is: http://www.crl.com/~mjr/thrower.html

For what Tony Brazelton calls, "The most extensive list of boomerang makers/venders on the web" head to http://staff.uiuc.edu/~brazelto/USBAinfo.html

Ted Bailey calls this, "The first web page you should visit." Other web sites recommended by Ted include:

http://ourworld.compuserve.com/homepages/Gerhard_Bertling/ and http://www.hal.com:80/services/juggle/help/circus-arts/boom/index.html as well as http:/www.jcn.com/mx/home.html

You can reach the publisher of 'BOUT BOOMERANGS at PLANTSpeak@AOL.com

And, as a final resource, always feel free to contact me at DarkPrint@AOL.com

Plenty of boomerang throwers bought their first returning sticks from Rich Harrison, apparently including Bud Pell:

STORAGE PROBLEMS

ONE HUNDRED FIFTY NOW
ON HAND
THERE'S NO MORE ROOM
FOR ME TO STAND.
ONLY ONE REASON I'M IN
THIS JAM;
BLAME IT ON THE
BOOMERANG MAN.

A Closing Dialogue

"Hey, did you check out Air Gorski's floater yesterday? " the man called out to the woman. "He's really shredding lately."

The woman cupped her ear to hear the man over the wind. She remembered him from the practice field yesterday, and he looked like a really dedicated boom competitor.

He had to be talking to her, because they were the only two people practicing in this crazy weather. It was hard to hear what he said, but he was probably asking her for some throwing advice. "Looks like your rang just blew by," she shouted back. "Keep it vertical, by the way — and use your tri-fly®!"

The man couldn't believe it. Was this woman actually trying to tell him how to throw? Him? He'd competed in boom tournaments all across the country, without any of her help, thank you very much. "Everybody's a critic," he grumbled, picking up his swiss cheese Omega instead.

"Watch this, then," he said to the woman, as he moved a little closer to her, picking a point just slightly higher than the horizon. "I'll guarantee you'll see a real rippa!"

The woman yawned. Geez, not another one of those kind of guys. He acted like Babe Ruth pointing his bat towards the stands. "You think you're such a boom stud," she said. "It'll just be another blow-by."

By now, the man was irritated with this woman. She sure didn't need to have such an attitude, not when he was only making conversation. "What makes you such a boom babe?" he asked, his hands on his hips.

"This," she said, whizzing a fast catch boom out 20 meters in the opposite direction of the man, then snagging a one handed catch. "About three or four seconds, wouldn't you say?"

The man was impressed. "Wow! That was incredible," he said. "Maybe you should be giving me some tips."

"You're as good as I am," she said, walking towards him. "That was an awesome dingle arm throw you made out there, by the way. I'm just nervous about tomorrow, competing against Gel, Chet the Jet, Broadboom, the Moleman and Chi Bob. This is my first national."

The man laughed, and he nodded his head in agreement. "I know what you mean. I'm afraid I'll toss some grounders tomorrow, while they make the raddest catches ever. I'm not even sure I want to try the Aussie Round or the MTA."

"Yeah, we'd better work together, instead of arguing," she agreed, figuring this guy wasn't so bad, after all. "What about adding a little flapage to the boom? Have you tried a humpback throw?"

Hey - like a boomerang, a book like this always ends up at the starting point — full circles to all of you! ...Kelly

Publisher's Comment

All across America we see evidence of the emergence of boomeranging as a popular sport. In parks and fields, even on beaches from the east coast to the west coast, bands of people are getting together to try their hand at tossing the stick that returns. As this book reflects, the sport has been active since the sixties. National and international competitions have been taking place since 1981. Members of the United States Boomerang Association have conducted their sports tournaments, for the most part out of sight of the general public and far away from the approving roar of the crowds of knowledgeable fans who follow other sports. So, it is true that boomerangers engage in their sport in a vortex of silence, for the most part unknown and unsung, except to their fellow enthusiasts. Boomerangers compete, for the most part, without sponsorship and without pay. At present, even the world championship competitions involve no cash prizes. All this may soon change. There is a serious drive to make the sport of boomeranging an Olympic event. The next Olympics will be held in the year 2000 in Sydney, Australia the continent most people associate with the birth of the boomerang. We hope, of course, that this book helps introduce to a larger public the sport of boomeranging and the names of the stars and the events at which they excel. We hope that the sport of boomeranging achieves the greater number of participants, both here in America and in other countries of the world, that it will take to qualify it as an Olympic event. Yet beyond that, we hope this book serves to help express that admirable spirit of the boomerang thrower, the beauty of a boomerang in flight, and the bond between nature and men and women that is established and somehow reinforced by the simple act of tossing "the stick that returns."

About the Author

A resident of Lorain, Ohio, freelance writer Kelly Boyer Sagert is a correspondent for the Lorain Morning Journal newspaper. Kelly has written over 60 magazine articles and is also the author-interviewer for America On-Line, where she interviews talented authors discussing their writing methods, backgrounds, current projects, and future plans. Kelly is a 1983 graduate of the Bowling Green State University with a BA in Psychology. After writing newspaper features on world class boomerang throwers Gary Broadbent and John Gorski, she started writing about boomerangs for magazines, including Boys' Life, Boys' Quest, People and Places and The Works Magazine. Earning a reputation as "the boomerang writer," she decided to actually start throwing boomerangs while writing this book. She and husband, Don, have two sons, Adam and Ryan. As a direct result of their mutual involvement in the writing of this book, Kelly and Don and photographer Len Burns started their own fledgling boomerang business called "Something Catchy."

Photograph Credits:

Cover Photographs: Front - Birds, Alan Scott Craig; Boomerang, Kim Deutschman; photo left: Chet Snouffer; photo top right: Snouffer Brothers; photo bottom right: Gary Broadbent

Back - Boomerangs left, top to bottom: Girvin, Bellen; Girvin, Rad; Deutschman; Mike Janke, Tri; Girvin, Sunshine; Boomerangs right, top to bottom: Girvin, Art Boom; Girvin, Deuce; Girvin, Carlotta; Girvin, Sunbell; Girvin, Sunset; from Ted Bailey collection.

Text: page #s 1,2: from Ted Bailey collection; 2: Modern 4-blade made by Girvin; 3,4,6 from Ted Bailey collection; 24: Photo by Jack Perkins; 29: Photo by Betsylew Miale-Gix; 32: Photo by Frances Van Kirk Flynn; 35: w/permission of Michael Girvin; 41,55: Photos by Bob Leifeld; 45: w/permission of John Anthony, 43,48,51,57: Photos by Angela Leifeld; 85,87,88,91,112: Photos of booms in Ted Bailey's collection; 90: w/permission of John Cryderman; 92: from Kim Deutschman collection, 93,94: slide collection from Neil Kalmanson, 96,97: w/permission of Alan Scott Craig; 103: Photo by Doug DuFresne